PAST: PERFECT!
PRESENT: TENSE!

PAST: PERFECT!
PRESENT: TENSE!

✦

Insights From One Woman's Journey As The Wife Of A Widower

Julie Donner Andersen

iUniverse, Inc.
New York Lincoln Shanghai

PAST: PERFECT! PRESENT: TENSE!
Insights From One Woman's Journey As The Wife Of A Widower

iUniverse, Inc.

For information address:
iUniverse, Inc.
2021 Pine Lake Road, Suite 100
Lincoln, NE 68512
www.iuniverse.com

This is in part a work of fiction. Although inspired by actual events, the names, persons, places, and characters are inventions of the author. Any resemblance to people living or deceased is purely coincidental.

ISBN: 0-595-27480-3

Printed in the United States of America

REVIEWS

"I recommend this book as a guide to avoid creating problems in a new remarriage. It will help prevent turning a relationship of two people into a triangle!"

—Anne K. Edwards, reviewer for eBook Reviews Weekly and author of *Journey Into Terror* (PublishAmerica).

*"...Andersen writes with both compassion and grace. Never afraid to touch the sensitive issues, she slowly but surely pulls the veil that has formerly covered the "taboo" subject of WOWs, and in so doing shares with us not only her story, but perhaps our own as well...**A wonderful resource** for not just WOWs but anyone experiencing the ups and downs of a blended family, or even coping with grief."*

—Rusty Fischer, contributing writer: *Chicken Soup for the Preteen Soul* (Health Communications, Inc.), *More Stories for a Woman's Heart* (Multnomah Press), and *A Cup of Comfort for Friends* (Adams Media).

*"I am glad to see that someone with real-life experience has penned a book that addresses the unique challenges of an often-overlooked group—Wives Of Widowers. This book is **a "must-have" for all WOWs** and an excellent resource for counselors, clergy and anyone else looking to expand their areas of empathy."*

—Susan Law Corpany, author of *Brotherly Love, Unfinished Business* and *Push On* (Hagoth Publishing Company, Inc.)

*"...Mrs. Andersen writes from the heart, with incredible insight, sensitivity, openness, humour, and an extraordinary understanding of the feelings of a widower. **She offers invaluable advice** (that) empowers the WOW, but the range of emotions expressed is equally as relevant to those who are living*

with someone who has lost any close relative, whether it is a wife, a husband, a child or a parent."

—Jan Andersen, freelance writer and host of *"World Writer"* website (**http://worldwriter.homestead.com**) and *"Mothers Over 40"* website (**http://www.mothersover40.com**).

"…With honesty, grace and clarity, Mrs. Andersen offers **a welcomed companion** for the often misunderstood and amazingly courageous wife of a widower."

—Karon Goodman, author of *The Stepmom's Guide to Simplifying Your Life* (EquiLibrium Press, Inc.).

"Julie Donner Andersen speaks from the heart; feelings moulded from her personal experiences. Her openness and willingness to share are refreshing. Ms. Andersen definitely has something to offer women in her same life situation. Her writing style is easy to read and offers specific support and her own proven personal methods of healing. Many how-to books have a stiff style with the author obviously lacking personal experience. This book is a welcome relief. **As a therapist I would and have recommended it to other wives of widowers.**"

—Raymond Mark, R.D; B.S.W; H.B.A. *Psychotherapist/Clinic Director; Ontario, Canada*

This book is dedicated to…

…my husband, Christian; my soul mate and best friend without whom I would not have had the inspiration to write it. Thank you for supporting me and giving me courage. I love you more than mere words could express.

…my children: Lindsay, Zachary, and Chelsea—the joys of my existence. Thank you for keeping me grounded. May the dreams you dream today become tomorrow's realities.

…my mother, Sue Donner; the rock of my life. Thank you for loving me through good times and bad, for believing in me, and for giving me wings. Your legacy of love will never be forgotten.

…my Lord and Savior, Jesus Christ; the One Who created love in the first place. Thank You…for everything. My life is Yours.

Contents

PREFACE

Why is a book about WOWs (Wives Of Widowers) necessary? Good question!

I decided to brave the previously uncharted waters of this particular genre of WOW information in the hope of uniting a special sisterhood of women who, like me, deal with issues, questions, emotions, hopes, dreams, and fears regarding marrying a man whose first wife has passed away, but who likely have no one to talk to about, or lack information regarding, the life upon which she is about to endeavor.

Since there is barely enough WOW (Wife Of a Widower) information and literature in libraries and bookstores to fill a thimble, the only resources I have used are the ones I trust the most—my own experiences and those of my fellow WOWs...because we know. We have lived it, and continue to live it every day—this up-and-down, roller-coaster ride of loving men who walk the journey of grief on a daily basis, but who have asked us to join them.

I believe that as human beings, we require validation for our feelings—the right to feel our feelings, no matter how bizarre others may find them—and WOWs are no exception. For WOWs, however, problems arise when getting that validation means the possibility of being perceived by others as completely selfish and unsympathetic. And the WOW often *does* stand a good chance of being judged harshly, since she is dealing not only with herself but with someone who has experienced the death of a spouse, as well as all of the people who have loved and lost the woman he once called his wife. Our WOW angst about the late wife, and issues that arise because of her, make us seemingly petty and unrealistic to the outside world, but nothing could be further from the truth.

We care deeply about the feelings of her survivors, and often about the late wife herself. But at the same time, we feel helpless and often hopeless in a society that still finds death and death-related issues "taboo". It is my hope that this book will help WOWs-to-be and newlywed WOWs find the peace of knowing that they are not alone, nor are they crazy for having WOW anxieties.

Of course, there will be WOWs who will never experience what this book describes. I cannot speak for all WOWs. I can, however, relate my experiences and those of WOW "sisters", advise you about the solutions that have worked for us, and hope that if you, as a WOW (or future WOW), can relate to or glean from this book, then its creation and the inspiration that I hope it may inspire in your life have not been for naught.

I am not a licensed social worker, psychologist or psychiatrist, or an expert. Therefore my observations about the WOW experience in this book should be considered only examples of what I and other WOWS have experienced ourselves. Please do not assume that any advice or opinions I offer are acknowledged, certified, or even widely accepted by the mental health community. It's just me talking to you, friend to friend and WOW to WOW…relating, complaining, laughing, crying, rejoicing, and sharing our thoughts, feelings, and insights together, hoping to grow from the bedrock of our mutual life experiences of being married to widowers.

Consider this book the validation you crave, with my blessing. It was written for you…

~Julie Donner Andersen

FOREWORD

To All Non-WOW Readers: From The Author

I am currently the happy wife of a wonderful man who lost a wife to cervical cancer when she was only 27 years old. I didn't know her, although I would like to have known the woman who my husband loved before me…and DURING me…as well as the life they shared together. Wouldn't YOU be curious?

Most second wives have the distinct pleasure of sizing up the "enemy" (the first or ex-wife) face to face. These encounters, though sometimes unpleasant, at least reassure the second wife of the reasons her husband decided to end the relationship with his ex, thus allowing the second wife to feel more confident in her husband's devotion to her alone. There are no "ghosts" in her marriage or her husband's heart since the ex wife, in all her glory, is the living, breathing validation of why he chose to start over and make a new life. But it's not like that for a "WOW" (Wife Of a Widower).

Allow me to illustrate by taking you on a virtual walk with me down WOW Lane. Try to picture the scenarios that I am about to describe.

Imagine your husband perhaps a decade younger than he is today. You see a pretty young woman holding his hand. They are chatting idly, perhaps sharing a park bench as they tell each other their dreams of the future. There are children playing nearby on the swing set. The young woman with your husband waves at the older couple pushing the swings. They are his wife's parents. They come over and embrace your husband warmly. After all, he is their son-in-law.

They then go to your husband's house, which is decorated in the style of his talented, pretty young wife. Family pictures with happy, smiling faces of a husband and wife and their children adorn the walls of the foyer. In the family room, their friends have gathered to have a drink and a laugh as they reminisce about "the good old days" when they were all young together. The pretty young woman moves closer to your husband, patting his hand with hers, and they share a glance that reminds the other of their happiness and the intimate dance of two intertwined souls.

After the gathering, the children are tucked into bed and kissed, and your husband is pleased that the children resemble the pretty young woman. She then signals to your husband in her feminine way that he knows so well that it's time for bed. They crawl into the sheets together, and snuggle close to each other in a sexy embrace that leads to lovemaking. Their marriage is good, and they seem to have everything going for them. They are, by all appearances, the perfect couple. Everyone says so, and many are jealous of their union being as wonderful as it is, until the worst happened.

Now, picture your husband with unmistakable fear in his eyes as a grim, faceless doctor delivers the fateful news of a terminal illness. His dreams, his life, his very soul is about to be taken from him prematurely, and there is nothing he or anyone else can do about it. The pretty young woman is going to die, he is told, and at that very moment, he wants to die, too. His anger and frustration are indescribable, but he tries desperately to remain focused on the task at hand—caring for the pretty young woman he loves more than life itself, until she draws her last breath.

You see him reduced to a shell of the man he once was…one who cleans up vomit from the bathroom floor after chemotherapy treatments…one who carries the pretty young woman, whose weak body is now a mere 80 lbs, to the bathtub and gently washes her as they talk about hope and remission…one who inserts another IV bag for his lifelong companion as he attempts a weak, tired smile at her—the skeleton of a woman lying in their bed. You can almost feel his heart breaking in two. You listen as he whispers yet another prayer that God take her away from all of this pain…but not too soon, as he doesn't think he's ready to live without her just yet.

Now, as hard as it may be, try to visualize your husband crying out in primal anguish, his wracking sobs sending shivers down your spine. You see the pretty young woman lying in a hospital bed, but she is no longer pretty. Cancer has taken her youth and her life from her, and her skin is gray and her eyes, cold. He is holding her lifeless hand, as a machine nearby delivers its death toll of a flat line. Your husband watches helplessly as the nurses draw a sheet up over the young woman's face…the final curtain on the drama that has been his life for a year. The pretty young woman's family comes to your husband and draws him close, as they share the intimate grief that only people who have lost a loved one to death can understand. They feel bonded, united, and sad beyond words.

Your husband musters up his last ounce of courage to deal with children who have lost the only mother they have ever known. He feels protective of them now more than ever. He mindlessly makes funeral arrangements, and his anger at the absurdity of choosing a casket that will hold the wife he cannot, only serves to bring more tears to his swollen eyes. You hear another prayer, this one barely audible, as he bargains with God for a miracle…that maybe his wife is really still alive but can't find a way to reach him, and he swears, "Oh, Lord, if You can only find a way to bring her back, I'll devote my life to You. I'll go to church every Sunday. I'll put more money in the basket, and I'll live every day to the fullest in gratitude for this miracle".

But the miracle doesn't happen the way he asks, and you watch as your husband retreats into his own private hell, trying to live each day one at a time, wondering if this gnawing ache in his heart will ever go away, hoping that some day, he will be able to get through a day without tears, or without passing by her pictures in the foyer and wanting to scream at the horror of her death and the agony of her loss. He hugs her pillow as he drags his hopeless body into bed, and smells her perfume on the pillowcase, trying to make the memory of her smiling face a permanent etching on his mind. He wonders about the meaning of his life, and he finds it hard to make sense of a world that keeps on spinning when all he wants to do is shrivel up and be cast into the wind like dust. Wanting her back is endless. Trying to rebuild his shattered life is a thought he pushes away. He likes the emotional cave of sorrow he lives in, for it serves as a monument to her life. He feels that as long as he can grieve for her and remain a hollow, empty soul, he has honored her and has not betrayed her memory. The only comfort he finds is in knowing that with each passing day, he is one step closer to being reunited with her in Heaven when his own life comes to a blissful end.

But life DOES go on, and you witness time becoming more of a friend to your husband. Years have passed, and he can now look at the pretty young woman's pictures and smile instead of cry. He can laugh now, without feeling guilty about living. Although a little older and a little grayer, he has put back the weight he lost during the time when food was unappetizing. Friends, who avoided his grief because they couldn't understand it, have started calling again, and their memories of his dearly departed keep her spirit alive in his heart.

But he is lonelier than he has ever been. It's not the company of other people he misses but the joy of a committed relationship and the benefits of living day to day in the company of a best friend. He has walked through the fires of hell, and has survived. His perseverance has strengthened his resolve to appreciate life more fully, and he has come to understand why God would not bargain with him. God knew what He was doing, and your husband doesn't blame God any more, because he realizes that to become the man YOU now love, he had to evolve and learn what life had to teach him…the good, the bad, and the ugly.

Your journey through the past as a "Virtual WOW" is over. How do you feel? Can you recall the many conflicting emotions you felt as I described your husband's past? Now admit it…wasn't the hardest part of your visualization trying to separate your own apparently selfish feelings from the pain of your husband's heart? Did you not feel a twinge of jealousy along the way, as well as overwhelming feelings of sorrow and helplessness towards the man you love?

Congratulations! You have somewhat successfully walked in the shoes of a WOW!

Because the late wives' deaths were such dramatic events in our husbands' lives, we WOWs come to know the story very well, and strangely enough, we share the grief they bear because of the emotional wreckage it left of the life we now share with him. Our hearts break with him, for him, and because of him. But all too often, our own anxieties about his past silence us. They force us to deny or hide our basic human need for acceptance and to be loved unconditionally and without comparison. His grief is huge and ever-present, becoming a strange priority in the marriage of not two hearts, but three.

What's it like to share your husband's heart with another woman, and be accepting of it…even encouraging of it? you may ask. Well, try to imagine a cloistered, remote tribe deep in Africa or somewhere else in the world where this might be an acceptable practice that is revered in high esteem. Brings to mind polygamy and all sorts of negative connotations, doesn't it? And yet, WOWs live with a similar version of this ideology each and every day of their lives.

WOWs are women who know they must accept the fact that they were not the first choice of their husband's heart in the marriage department. Surreal as it sounds they also accept that they wouldn't be married to their men if the late wives had lived. These are hard pills to swallow. Every new bride wants her husband to make her feel uniquely his and no one else's—special beyond comparison—and most are confident they are #1 in their husbands' heart, barring all others. Even if he had the most checkered past, a non-widower's heart now belongs only to his new wife.

Everyone has a past. We women have all had boyfriends who we were hopelessly devoted to, only to watch the relationship crash and burn, whether it was our choice to end it or not. But WOWs live with the fact that their husband's marriages did not end badly, nor was the parting of he and his late wife something either of them wanted. There was no option…fate chose FOR them.

All of this knowledge leads to much anxiety and insecurity on the part of the WOW. On one hand, she feels deep sympathy for the anguish her husband has endured, and wants to be his helpmate in his grief journey as much as she can. But on the other hand, her self-doubt grows with each memory that triggers grief for her husband.

She wonders about this thing called bereavement—will he ever truly "get over it" or "get beyond it"? Her self-esteem suffers, as she fears that she may never be the true love of her husband's life. Shamefully, she rages at the ghost of his late wife for being ever-present in her marriage, and starts to resent this woman's prior existence on this planet and in her husband's heart.

The WOW's competitive nature forces her to try to out-do the late wife in many ways, hoping to earn that spot on the pedestal the late wife occupies and knock her off completely. She loves her husband so much and truly wants to be patient, but she tires quickly of playing the grief therapist. Feelings of selfishness nag at her soul, as she hungers for autonomy apart from the memories of "her" that her husband holds near and dear. Yet she still thirsts for knowledge of the woman from her husband's past that she never knew…perhaps to visualize the late wife as more "real" and human, and perhaps to strengthen her edge of the competition should the late wife's reality pale in comparison to her own. *Maybe if I discover that the late wife had some faults and failures, I could feel more superior and more worthy*, she desperately thinks.

Drearily, the competition becomes a battle of "one step forward, two steps back", with no end in sight. The WOW wants so badly to purge the thoughts of her husband and his late wife from her mind, but still stays awake at night with self-pity as her closest companion, constantly struggling with visions whose insanity scares her—thoughts of her husband reunited with his late wife in heaven…wondering if he longs for his late wife's body instead of her own…wishing "their song" would disappear from radio air play…wondering what he's thinking about her at which given time…feeling totally inept and unworthy of his love and devotion as she fights the demons she fears will destroy her new marriage before it's begun.

Yet there is no one to whom the WOW can vent her negative feelings of fear, frustration, guilt, shame, and anger because of her paranoia of being viewed as a selfish, unsympathetic, and insensitive shrew. Perhaps, at one time, she felt proud of being the heroine in her husband's saga, and now discovers that her white steed was nothing more than a sluggish mule. Society itself regards her as a mere replacement, and has no tolerance for her confused feelings. Perhaps he won't even discuss his late wife or their marriage with her, making the WOW feels more insecure (since the fear of the unknown is the greatest fear of all!). She feels like the stranger…the intruder…the "other woman"…in her own marriage. She is on the outside looking in…and she has never felt lonelier.

Friends and family from the past are cautious with the WOW, unsure of how to handle her, so they don kid gloves while helplessly comparing her every move to that of their dearly departed loved one. The WOW is aware of this, and is self-conscious in their presence. She is saddened by the thought that no one can accept her for the unique and special person she is APART from their memories of the woman whose life is easily recalled by those who loved her. So she grins and grimaces when they accidentally call her by the late wife's name, or spin their tales of funny memories of their mutual past in uproarious laughter. Once again, she is the outsider. Even new people she meets are curious about her husband's prior life and former wife, again relegating the WOW to second place in every conversation.

But just like with grief, time becomes her friend. The years pass, and the WOW learns to accept the things she cannot change. Life teaches her that the woman she once resented helped to forge the character of the man she loves. She forgives herself and offers and olive branch to the late wife's memory. She begins to heal, and starts living in the present more and more, thus bringing her husband along with her into this newfound hope for the future. By doing so, her fears are squelched, as her husband reassures her that his love for her is true, beautiful, hopeful, and ever growing. He begins to appreciate her individuality and the gifts she brings to his life. By sharing his heart with the late wife, the WOW comes full circle to the knowledge that the late wife is not and has never been a threat but a sweet memory of a life. Even her husband admits that he has evolved away from his past, in so much as his life experiences have changed him into a different man…the man the WOW fell in love with in the first place.

Friends and family become more accepting, perhaps because time worked its magic for their grief journeys as well, and they begin to enjoy the uniqueness of the new WOW. She and her husband make new friends…people who are clueless about her husband's former life…and the couple begin making memories that have nothing do with the past or anyone from it.

So, what is a WOW? It depends on what part of the journey she is on, but I CAN tell you the person she *will* become at the end of the long WOW road to recovery: flawed and human, but always empathetic and self-sacrificial, she is a woman of great courage, strength, and perseverance, as she makes her way through the darkness of her fear into the light of hope. She is selfless, accommodating, sympathetic, and gracious, as she shares her husband's love with another woman and makes room in her marriage for her husband's grief. She has learned that "standing by your man" does not mean standing by his late wife so much as supporting *him* as *he* does. She believes in the healing powers of love and time, as she reminds herself and her husband to live in the present and embrace life with gusto.

But most of all, she believes wholeheartedly in her marriage, her man…and herself. Her faith stares down the demons, and she emerges once again as the heroine on a white steed…this time, in the story of her ***own*** life.

HOW LONG IS 'LONG ENOUGH'?

A widowed friend of mine fell in love with a man she had known throughout her entire twenty-five year marriage, two months after her spouse's death from terminal cancer. She confided to me that while she would probably never get over her husband's death, her grief was now "manageable". She mentioned that during her husband's yearlong fight to survive, her overwhelming duties as his caretaker had plunged her into an early grief long before her husband actually drew his last breath. She felt confident that she had reached a point in her grief journey where her heart could make room for both her new love and her memories of her late husband.

However, friends and family alike clucked their judgmental tongues and warned her that two months was not long enough for her to have come to grips with her loss. They concluded that my friend's new relationship was "transitional" at best, and that her feelings for the new man in her life couldn't possibly be real. They decided that her grief must have rendered my friend lonely and confused, and assumed that she couldn't be ready to love again so soon after her tragic loss. Finally, they determined that by openly parading her new relationship around town, my friend was acting irresponsibly and insensitively to her late husband's memory. They felt her actions were downright shameful.

My friend soon ended her relationship with her new love, but not because she felt that she was stuck in a stage of the grief cycle, or because she stopped loving him. She just couldn't bear the lack of support, the negative reactions to her happy news, and the pointing and whispering that went on behind her back. She died six months later, brokenhearted and alone.

I can relate to my late friend's fear of negative societal response. When I met my previously widowed husband, his wife had been gone for almost three years. While he was certain within his own heart and mind that he was mentally and emotionally prepared to rejoin the living and move on with his life, his circle of supposed supporters were just as quick to admonish him. Three years, they decided, was not a suitable timeframe in which to complete the grief cycle, and cast a deciding vote against not only his new life, but also on me as his new love interest.

I believed that by the three-year mark, my then-boyfriend would have already dealt with his grief issues to everyone's satisfaction. I naively judged that three years was definitely the "kosher" amount of time for someone to lose a spouse, do some grieving, and move beyond bereavement into the dating scene again. Imagine my shock to learn that in some peoples' opinion, in total opposition of my own, three years was like a drop of water in an ocean of time.

So who was right? Were my husband's friends correct to disapprove of his three year waiting period? Was it accurate for me to assume that three years was long enough? And what about my late friend? Was two months not long enough to complete her personal grief journey and find love again? And if not, then how long IS "long enough"?

Our society is made up of people with vastly differing opinions. One person's definition of "right/enough" is another person's judgment of "wrong/not enough". Therefore, a standard against which to measure the appropriateness of a widow or widower's readiness to rejoin the dating pool does not really exist. Grief is an emotion, and as with all emotions, grief has no boundaries, nor does it come with its own timetable or set of rules.

Like any other emotion, grief is neither "right" nor "wrong"—it just *is*. While three years may be the "suitable" amount of time for some survivors' grief cycles to come full circle, it is definitely not "long enough" for other widows or widowers. But one thing is for sure—*only the man or the woman who is struggling to move beyond bereavement can make that determination.* No one else can, or should, make it for them.

Society bases its judgments on its own comfort level, and inevitably makes sweeping generalizations based upon them. If we are not comfortable with bi-racial marriage, then we claim it is "wrong". If we are unnerved by homosexuality, then we shout from the rooftops that it is a "deviant lifestyle". When people allow ignorance to cloud their rational thought, which in turn leads them outside of their comfort zones, the resulting concrete judgments make everyone suffer. Compassion, tolerance, and acceptance are then damned to the wayside.

This same theory appears to hold water in regard to widows and widowers who wish to re-enter the dating world. Society is simply not adequately informed about the totality of grief, but still allows this ignorance to cast stones at the widow/er for contemplating dating or remarriage.

To its benefit, perhaps society does so to protect its weakest at the most vulnerable time in its members' lives. We do not like standing idly by and watching a broken spirit be taken advantage of, nor do we want such a fragile heart to be hurt again, so we rush in to defend a widow/er's honor in the name of protecting him/her from making a mistake. However, in doing so, we disregard that widow/er's personhood and assume that they are far too grief-stricken to formulate rational thoughts and decisions, thereby confusing the bereaved even further and causing "fits and starts" in what otherwise might be a healthy new relationship with a new partner.

Perhaps we, as a society, are skeptical of widow/er remarriage because those of us who have had long and happy marriages cannot even begin to fathom doing so ourselves should we ourselves ever lose our spouses. It is hard to guess how we would react within the realm of grief, much less if we would consider loving again, while walking through its stages. But therein lies the rub. We cannot make assumptions about something or someone we know nothing about unless or until it happens to us personally. And even then, no grief journeys are the same.

What society fails to recognize about the journey of grief is that people grieve in their own distinct ways, and in their own differing lengths of time. No two grieving individuals share the same grief journey because they, like people themselves, are unique to each person. To make judgments about the move beyond bereavement being "too soon" or "long enough", without ever having personally stepped a foot on the path of grief, is like opining about giving birth when you have never been pregnant. Sure, you could read the literature and make an intelligent speech about the *mechanics* of the birth process, but you would not be viewed as credible when speaking of the *mental and emotional aspects* of carrying and delivering a child. Only a birth mother could do that.

It would seem to follow, then, that fellow widows and widowers would understand their counterparts and give them latitude in regard to loving again or wanting to remarry, no matter what the length of time between loss and newfound love. Ironically, though, other widows and widowers who have yet to find new love, or could care less about finding it, are often the least supportive of their fellow loss survivors who are already standing at the ready on the springboard of new love.

One possible explanation of this is known as "The Pedestal Effect". Grief researchers and scholars have noted that most widow/ers experience a period during grief where they "canonize" their late spouse's memory, thereby placing the deceased on a pedestal too high for anyone to approach.

In this stage of grief development, the bereaved can only remember that his/ her late spouse was perfect in every way, and that no one could ever "take his/her place". A new love interest that may be compared to this unattainable standard of perfection is doomed to pale. Many widow/ers feel that they must remain single/ widowed to preserve the memory of their late spouse. This act is self-sacrificial in nature, but is often the antithesis of personal growth. To these particular widow/ers, loving again is akin to dishonoring a deceased's memory, and they can be very critical of another widow/er who dares to defame their own respective "saint".

To love again after loss takes an extreme amount of courage, considering the obstacles that stand in the way of a widow/er's own personal happiness. However, if you are a survivor who has been alone for either a few weeks or several decades and are wondering what the answer to the question "How long is 'long enough'?" might be, I can tell you without hesitation—it's whenever *YOU* decide the time is right.

1

THE SISTERHOOD OF WOWS

When I started dating my previously widowed husband, I wanted to learn all I could about grief (for which there are thousands of references on the Internet and millions of books pertaining to the subject) in order to better empathize with his plight. But mostly, I wanted to be a more compassionate and truly sympathetic marriage partner. For that, love is not enough. Knowledge, in this respect, is key.

My research completed, I then had some information to help me understand the journey of grief and the pain of loss through death (which, I discovered, was something no one really understands fully unless or until it happens to them personally).

However, after endless hours of searching for information about being a second wife to a widower and all the issues that that entails, I was frustrated to discover that none existed. Was this a subject that was so delicate and fraught with emotion that no one had dared pen a manuscript to help women who were contemplating becoming wives of widowers deal with the psychological drama that was about to become their marriages?

The Problem Of Compartmentalizing WOWs

I have had the pleasure of corresponding with fellow WOWs regarding our mutual issues while researching this book. By doing so, to my surprise, I have discovered a new perspective.

One new WOW "sister" was surprised to learn of the vast array of WOW problems, claiming that she personally had not dealt with nary ONE of them, and insisting that she felt secure in her acceptance, that the past was the past, and that her husband's late wife was never an issue in her marriage or in her heart. I was absolutely enthralled by her courage.

But I also pessimistically pondered, "Oh, really? How could this be? Perhaps I am jumping the gun in writing this book for *all* WOWs. Don't all of us WOWs walk the same walk? Aren't we all in the same boat? Is it possible that our individuality or differing life experiences make us altogether different WOWs, too?"

Just as all people are different, so are all WOWs. Some of us came into this marriage with children, some didn't. Some of us have had a child with our widowed husbands, and some have not. Some of us were prior single women, and some of us had been married before. Some of us have major problems with the late wife's friends and family, and some of us don't. And the list goes on.

Because of these special differences, we each apparently handle the tough WOW issues in unique ways, depending on our individual characters and life experiences from which we invoke the wisdom needed to get us through the hard times and make us appreciate the good times.

The Ties That Bind

While all of these factors might appear to separate us WOWs, there is still one fact that bonds us. No, it is not the insecurity we feel at times. No, it is not the "haunted" feelings. And no, it is not even the fact that we are all married to previously widowed men, although that would appear to be the most common sense answer.

It is this: we are all WOMEN! Unique in life experiences and individuality, we all share the same gender, and as such, the common bond that unites a special alliance of people. We are not POWs (people of widowers)…the first "W" means "wives"; women; married women; sharing a common experience of being married to the last "W"—widowers. But, first and foremost: women!!

I believe that being a woman married to a previously widowed man is unique, yet special, in and of itself. A man can marry a widow (would they then be called HOWs?), and deal with a few of the same issues common to WOWs, and I certainly hope that husbands of widows could relate to this book as much as WOWs could. But as women, our issues are slightly different just for the simple fact that we *are* women. Generally speaking, we, as a gender, are more sensitive to other people's feelings, *sometimes at the expense of our own*. We are more aware of how the world perceives us, and we are hurt when the world's people do not see us as we would like them to. We sometimes tend to "over analyze" our thoughts and those of others, and our emotions run high when we assume too much negativity about our place in the world and how we "fit in".

My new WOW friends have concluded from our discussions that it is neither right nor wrong to have to (or NOT have to) deal with WOW issues, nor is it neither right nor wrong as to what degree we may each feel threatened (or NOT threatened) by the late wife. In accepting this viewpoint, I have also concluded something valuable, too: We are women—learning from each other, sharing with each other, and bonding because of that unspoken trust that accompanies female friendships, no matter what road we walk.

Sisterhood is a wonderful word. It brings to mind a comfortable sense of belonging. And I am proud and honored to be part of this fascinating "family" of WOWs—no matter what boat we share, and no matter how weak or strong we are in coping.

"WOW"—Another Definition of "Hero"

When we are asked about what defines a hero, many of us quickly reference the brave men and women who risked their lives, and lost them, in the World Trade Center tragedy—the firefighters, policemen, and average citizens who valiantly persevered, despite the odds against them, so that others might be saved. These people embody the true meaning of heroism to its extreme definition, and we are all the better for their existence on this planet. Their bravery and sacrifice of their own lives have made all Americans more patriotic, more compassionate, and most of all, more confident about the altruism that exists in the heart of man.

These heroes left behind hundreds of widows and widowers; people who are picking up the pieces of their shattered lives and trying to make sense of a tragedy that was senseless…many who are perhaps even trying in vain to explain such a loss to children who cannot understand that Mommy/Daddy is not coming home again. Our hearts break for them, and try as we may to understand their tremendous loss, we cannot—unless we ourselves have, at one time, lost a beloved spouse to death.

I have watched the television interviews with the young widows and widowers of the WTC disaster as they proudly honor their deceased spouses, and I am touched and saddened by their losses.

But as a WOW (Wife Of a Widower) myself, what also tears at my heart is the concern I have for the future wives and husbands who may remarry these bereaved young men and women, and the inevitable comparisons they will face from society—and even close to home.

It has been written by grief researchers and scholars that it is quite common and normal for a widow/er to hold his/her deceased spouse on a pedestal. These knowledgeable professors and doctors of science call this phenomena "canonization". In other words, a widow/er tends to remember only that his/her lost spouse was perfect in every way, thus making anyone else, by comparison, seem insignificant and unable to compete with such a virtuous person.

Fortunately, the same scholars tell us that this stage of grief is brief, and more than likely occurs during the first few years of bereavement—after which, the bereaved person begins to accept the loss, and his/her memories of the dearly departed become clearer and more realistic. That's good news for anyone who dares to date, fall in love with, or even marry, a widow/er. After all, it's hard to compete with such a "saint" or follow in the footsteps of a hero.

The widow/ers of the WTC tragedy face enormous fallout from their losses, but I imagine an even larger hurdle for them would be falling in love with someone else—someone whom they will feel will be good enough for, or better than, the epic heroes who will forever reside in their hearts.

Marrying a widow/er does not necessarily mean that a competition with his/her late spouse is inevitable, but I believe that most second spouses prefer knowing that the covetous place in their beloved spouses' hearts could be shared equally and without mental reservation or comparison.

However, in the case of marrying someone who lost a not only a spouse but a world hero, my first thought is, "What a tough act to follow!" Will the pedestals these young widow/ers place their heroic departed spouses upon ever become realistic enough to accommodate a new person to love? When opportunity comes knocking on their doors in the form of new love, will they make room in their hearts for the possibility, accepting the new lovers for who and what they are, without comparison, and fairly give them a chance? And will the new lovers ever work through the difficult task of keeping insecurities and self-doubt at bay when the world reminds them of the paragons of virtue that preceded them?

Loving and marrying a widow/er is no easy task, especially when you must accept that the man or woman you have vowed to love and support forever shares his/her heart with someone else.

That, in and of itself, makes all second spouses of the bereaved very brave souls.

These are people who, because of their great love and devotion, will willingly, compassionately, and selflessly accommodate their bereaved partners' memories and love for the spouses who came before them, thereby becoming helpmates in a shared grief that is respected and honored.

WOWs are truly representative of a different definition of heroism at its best and most hopeful.

2

WHAT TO EXPECT

While you may or may not relate to the following examples of expectations and insecurities, I believe that they are worthy of mention simply because they seem to be the most common feelings among WOWs I have known, myself included:

Expect The Transition to Take Time and Patience

I always caution WOWs-to-be that the first year is the hardest, and that "WOWdom" is NOT for the faint of heart, weak-willed, or impatient! For example, during this early, foundation-building time in your marriage, you may hear the late wife's name called out by him instead of yours, which may rock your trust in his grief recovery. You may find it hard to talk to your husband or husband-to-be about wills, funerals, or anything else death-related, and he may shy away from these types of discussions. You may find that he refuses to discuss his late wife at all, thinking that any mention of her may hurt you—something he is loathe to do because he loves you.

It is also possible, especially if he was his late wife's caretaker during her terminal illness, that he is overly health-conscious, or obsessive about your comings and goings since he doesn't want to lose you, either. He may be extremely affectionate, having done without for a long time, or he may be somewhat cold and standoffish, unable to cope with his guilt about betraying his late wife by loving again. He may be moody and depressed one day, happy-go-lucky the next.

Once you learn about grief and its aspects, you will find that these behaviors are quite normal for a widower, and as a WOW, you should try very hard not to take any of them personally. Hard as it may be to fathom, they really don't have anything to do with you. They are the knee-jerk reactions of a man who is trying to figure out, one day at a time, how to get some control and order back into his emotionally disorganized and upturned life.

Patience is key. Compassion is a given. Understanding is a duty. And love is a prerequisite to all.

Expect To Feel Threatened By A "Ghost"

The WOW often feels as if the late wife is a constant presence—in her home, her marriage, and even in her husband's heart. While it may appear to be an almost insane thought to those outside of WOWdom since the late wife is no longer alive to present much of a viable threat, these insecure feelings are nevertheless very real to the WOW.

Perhaps "her" pictures still adorn his walls. Perhaps "her" clothes still hang in "their" closet. Perhaps, if they had children together, the kids look like "her". Or perhaps you are sleeping in the same bed that "they" shared together.

These things, and the common feelings that accompany them, represent reminders to the WOW (or future WOW) that maybe her husband really isn't "over" his late wife (which he will never be), and therefore may never allow his new wife to occupy a similar place in his life or in his heart (which, of course, you will!), and may never fully commit himself 100% to the new marriage (although he is most certainly able to do so!)

Also, A WOW may feel that she is in competition with a "ghost", which is really her husband's memory of his late wife. There may be areas—such as character traits, talents, or outer beauty—where she does not compare herself favorably, and other areas where she may excel over the ghost. She may feel inadequate about not measuring up to her, and superior when you exceed the late wife in any trivial way.

I am here to tell you that your feelings and fears are normal and human, and are apparently validated by a majority of other WOWs. You are not crazy or selfish…and you are not alone.

Common Insecurities and Other WOW Issues

The following are just a few "crazy" (by society's standards) WOW thoughts, feelings, and issues that are common to new WOWs or WOWs-to-be:

—wondering if you'll ever be #1 in your husband's heart.

—feeling guilty about having these petty feelings, and/or feeling guilty about the selfishness of your feelings.

—feeling guilty about living another woman's life, or living the life the late wife would be living had she not died.

—not comparing favorably when others judge you, even when self-imposed.

—thinking that "she" was prettier, and/or younger, than you.

—thinking that if "she" walked in the door today, your husband would run to her.

—thinking that if you and "she" stood side by side and asked him to choose, he would choose "her".

—knowing that will never happen, and yet still feeling insecure about it.

—wondering which songs on the radio were "their" songs.

—wondering what triggers a fond memory of "her" to him—and how to avoid them.

—wondering how their sex life was and how you compare.

—cringing every time an anniversary of "theirs" or "her" birthday or death anniversary rolls around, and feeling sad for him when they do roll around.

—wanting to ask him about "her", but not sure you can deal with his answers.

—hoping time will make "her" memory fade even more.

—hoping he loves you more than he ever loved "her".

—wishing he never met or married "her"

—wishing he never had to go through so much pain when "she" died.

—wondering, when he gets that "far off look" in his eyes, if he is thinking of "her".

—dreading going anywhere "they" have been to before.

—dreading re-living old memories, with "you" as the role of "her".

—dreading doing any of the things that "they" used to do for fear of triggering another memory.

—hoping your memories together will outshine "theirs".

—wanting to hate "her" to justify your petty feelings, but not being able to because she died and didn't ask to.

—wanting to know more about "her", but not having anyone to ask.

—knowing you COULD ask him, but fearing that would lead to tears.

—wondering about his dying before you, and knowing that "they" will then reunite in Heaven while you are left to grieve.

—knowing that if he goes before you, no one will be there at Heaven's door to welcome you when it's your turn to go.

—wondering where he would want to be buried…by "her" or by you?

—not wanting to go through Eternity with "her" sharing him with you.

—feeling this awful burden of this Grief Monster on a daily basis.

—knowing that not a day goes by that "she" does not cross your mind, and wondering if "she" crosses his mind daily, too.

If it seems apparent that these observations are based on the individual WOW's insecurity, perhaps it is because they are. Surprisingly, self-esteem is not usually lacking in most WOWs. But insecurity, in essence, comes from a lack of assurance, reaffirmation, and validation: that wonderful support which may be sorely lacking in the life of a WOW.

Expect Your Husband's Grief to Co-Exist with His Love For You

No matter how long or how shortly they were married, the widower has experienced a devastating blow. All at once, his dreams were shattered, the love of his heart was taken from him prematurely, and he had no control over any of it. He may have still been walking in the early stages of his grief journey when you met him. He may always walk it to some degree. Grief has no timetable. But one thing is for sure—widows and widowers NEVER "get over it". They just learn how to cope over time. And, as harsh as it may sound, the sooner you learn to accept this fact, the stronger your marriage to a widower will be.

I believe that a widower will always experience grief in differing degrees, depending on various factors, for the rest of his life. But it IS reassuring to know that his feelings about his loss will not diminish the love he has for you! There are occasions when his grief will be stronger than other times, but the WOW who understands her husband's need to "feel and deal", while at the same time sacrificing her personal feelings about it, will be rewarded. What I mean is simply this: a person experiencing grief needs to feel it in order to deal with it. To ignore it or pretend it doesn't exist only fuels the fires of grief and makes it harder to move beyond bereavement.

In doing my research for this book, I met widows and widowers who, amazingly, expressed the hope that they would find love again, wanting to remarry. They hoped that a future spouse would embrace their lost loves, and understand that it IS possible to have loved, lost, and discover love the second time around can be even more special. They believed in the possibility that they could still love the deceased spouse while, at the same time, feel true, committed love for the next spouse. These hurting people dreamed of a future spouse who would not feel threatened or insecure about their love, as they felt sure they could love again in the same capacity that they had before. They wanted, more than anything, a future spouse who could understand that grief CAN co-exist with newfound love.

I truly believe that it is possible to have more than one soul mate in life. Just as a mother never negates the love she has for her first child by having another, so a widower also has enough love to embrace both his late wife and his present wife. And just as a mother loves all of her children the same, but also for their unique and individual personalities, so also does a widower feel for the wives in his life, past and present.

This is not to say that you need to embrace the late wife in some kind of strange sisterhood, or obsess about her so much that it stifles your life. But she should not be perceived as the enemy, either. She didn't do anything wrong...she just died. Acknowledge that she loved your husband, and he, her. Keep in mind that she helped to make him the man you love today, either positively or negatively, even if for whatever reasons their marriage was not that great. Be as supportive as you can comfortably be of the times when your husband feels the need to pay his respects on special grief-related occasions, for they have no negative impact on his love for you.

Expect To Be Taken Seriously

While busying yourself with meeting his grief needs, you may feel at times that your own needs are being ignored, and you may start to resent being such a dutiful WOW. This may happen especially if you are being compassionate in spite of your invalidated feelings, or if you are playing the WOW role with so much empathy that you are going without your own needs being met.

I don't mean to dissuade you with this book by saying that you must put aside your seemingly selfish, irrational, insecure WOW feelings for his sake because of his grief. Certainly not! You are entitled to ALL of your feelings, no matter how bizarre they may seem to you or to others. You are half of this marriage. You and your WOW feelings are as integral and as important as he and his grief. You are the present, the "here and now"; therefore, your feelings are worthy of validation and sensitivity. In short, you have a RIGHT to be heard and understood!

Being a WOW is not what makes you uniquely you, just as being a previous widower is not what your husband is all about, either. Widowhood and WOW-dom are just small pieces of your unique marriage puzzle. To make WOW issues or grief issues the entire focus of your marriage is a crutch, and you are asking for trouble if you are stifling your feelings and needs just because you don't want to burden your bereaved husband with them!

Sometimes, a widower is just plain confused and perplexed by his new wife's seemingly hateful or defiant attitude about the late wife. *How can my wife feel so threatened by "her" (the late wife) when she's not even here to defend herself?* he may think. Being the keeper of her memory, he becomes threatened by his new wife's inability to embrace her or love her as much as he did/does, which fuels the resentment fires. A widower who refuses to listen to his new wife's issues does nothing to help his new marriage grow. This is a learning process for BOTH of you—he must learn to respect your feelings and subsequent boundaries where the late wife is concerned, and he must learn to take them seriously, since they will impact the marriage in a big way.

For example, your husband suggests a vacation, yet it's the same place where he and his late wife spent their honeymoon. You have mixed feelings about this. As a WOW, your concern is that he may get there and trigger a memory that will then cause grief to follow, thereby ruining the good time you have looked forward to. In his mind, he only wants to take you there because he enjoyed the place in the past, and cannot understand why you are being so stubborn about not going.

Your husband must respect your fears as real to you. And you, in return, must try to accept it when what he tells you is an honest statement of fact about his feelings. The first step to being taken seriously is communication, coupled with compassion and respect for your mutual feelings without judgment. This will help guide you through the times of indecision that are based on fear of the unknown.

3

LIVING WITH THE PAST

"Dear Widowers…"

So many of us WOWs apparently have a deep desire to be reassured by our husbands that we are #1 with them, barring all others (including the late wife!). And many WOW husbands are gracious enough to answer our competitive questions regarding how we compare to the dearly departed by responding, "Yes, dear, *you* are the greatest lover in this world!" or "Yes, dear, *your* meat loaf is the best on the planet!"

Tactful, yes…but do these answers from our husbands really appease us? Do we not see through this clever disguise and come to realize that '*in this world*' and '*on the planet*' have nothing to do with the *heavenly, non-planetary* realm which house the late wives' souls, leaving "her" out of the comparison…and therefore, a widower's answer…altogether?

Why do we WOWs have such a great need to hear from our husbands that we are superior in every way to their late wives? *Why* is this competition so intense, especially when we know deep inside that there will be no winners at the end of this absurd "game"? And *why* is it of such paramount importance to know that our cooking abilities, sexual prowess, or other wifely skills, are *BETTER* than those of the women who came before us?

Simple—because we are *human*. However, the late wife is not, and her absence from this world and this planet leads many WOWs to draw their own conclusions and assumptions about their places in their husbands' hearts…especially since he is tactful, if not evasive, about how he speaks of his late wife and her humanness.

Second wives of divorced men accept that at one time, their husbands were happy with their ex wives, so there ARE memories of a time when all was good. However, these second wives can be reassured—just because of their husbands' divorces—that their men *chose* to part from their exes, and that there were usually fireworks of bad feelings at the end of those marriages. Because of the divorces, there is also the comforting confirmation that these husbands did NOT wish to spend the rest of their lives, much less eternity, with the shrews they left behind. The second wife of a divorced man has the pleasure of seeing for herself the reasons her husband chose to leave, as the ex is on display in all her glory for the present wife to behold—and it's often not a pretty picture.

However, the WOW lives with the fact that her husband did not choose to end his marriage. And while there may have been bad memories of the late wife's final days of anguish and pain, it was not the marriage relationship that endured any suffering. In fact, the intimacy shared by a widower and his dying wife, because of its intensity, cannot be duplicated, and becomes quite a heavy burden for the WOW, knowing that she may never achieve such closeness with her mate just because she draws breath daily.

The late wife is not physically present for the WOW to behold and gain confidence about her position in her husband's heart like a wife of a divorced man can. The WOW does, however, feel the late wife's presence in her home, her marriage, and in her husband's memory constantly. She may also hear about the "saint" that preceded her from family and friends. Because of these reasons, her feelings of inadequacy and her competitive spirit thirst to be quelled and quenched, but she has no one—except her husband—to help her to do that…and he's too busy trying to be diplomatic to really reassure his new wife to her complete satisfaction.

To that end, I wish to address remarried widowers in an open letter to all of them, hoping that it will give voice to WOWs who cannot bring themselves to broach the subject of "*What I Need You To Understand About My Being A WOW, And What I Need To Hear From You…No Matter How Stupid You May Find It*" with their men:

Dear Remarried Widowers,

First, let me say that no one can truly understand what you have endured by losing a beloved spouse to death, nor the agony of taking the frustrating "one step forward, two steps back" movements along your journey through bereavement. If we were to put ourselves in your shoes just for one tiny moment, our hearts would break in half just thinking about how terribly wracked with pain we, as wives, would be to lose you, our husbands. But it is only an assumption based on our deep love for you. You have experienced it, and therefore, deserve our utmost respect and sympathy for your loss.

But loving someone who grieves the loss of a wife is no easy task, no matter how far removed from the date of her death. However, we want to be there for you to undertake the role of helpmate throughout your journey. Our deep, abiding love is steadfast and strong, so you needn't feel like you must hide your memories. We have no desire to make you forget the life or wife who came before, for we know that to truly walk the stages of grief and come out on the "other side", you must be comfortable with talking about your past. Turn to us—we have broad shoulders, big ears, and warm hearts!

Ah, but you are afraid that speaking of the past will hurt us, thus making any mention of it a risk. But be bold, my friends! We might sting with the all-too-human pain of jealousy or insecurity, but bigger than those fears is the love we have for you and our desire to ease your transitions. You must understand that our fear of the unknown causes us much more anxiety than knowing that your late wives—and your love for them—were real and human and beautiful in your eyes.

But remember that we are weak with the hunger to know that your love for us is not diminished in any way by your grief or your memories. Be gentle with your affirmations and reassurances when our competitive natures forces us to ask you to be the judge and convey to us that we are not only special people but #1 in your hearts, should we feel inadequate in our own failed comparisons.

It must sound so silly to you, hearing that we long to be your late wives' replacements on their lofty pedestals. But wear our shoes for a moment…if you knew that we shared our hearts with the love and the memories of lovers who came before you, would you not also vie for that coveted place in our hearts? Would you not want to be assured that you are the loves of our lives? Would you not be uncomfortable with your spouses' silence…that unmistakable wall that leads to insecurity…leaving you to wonder if our thoughts were not with or about you, but with and about the men who once filled our hearts?

Many of you simply tell us WOWs to just "get over it", but can you see how absurd that statement is when you compare it to those who once told you the same thing about your grief? Did you not want to shake them, and remind them that if it were that easy, you'd be there by now? My friends, dear remarried widowers, we WOWs are the "here and now". We accommodate your grief and your memories like no other category of wife in the world would dare. And it is because of our love for you that we solemnly sit in the background and wait for our chance to shine in your hearts because, frankly, there is nowhere else we would rather be. We choose to share your love with the love of your past because doing so ensures us that place in your lives, now and in the future.

But it cannot always be about you and your grief. We cannot forget about your past any more than you can. We have needs, too…as human beings, as women, and as WOWs. We tire easily of playing the grief therapist only when your pain starts to make us feel hopeless about our own futures with you. We strive for that acceptance from you, that autonomy—apart from your late wives' memories—that will help us to feel that you are completely satisfied with not only what we are, but also who.

We married you not to step into your late wives' shoes nor to "become" these women, but to stake our own claim and make our own lives and memories with the men of our dreams. And no matter what kind of baggage you carry, it is our desire to help you ease the load if, in return, we can expect to feel worthy of your love and devotion to only us.

We do not ask much, and we sympathize and understand more than you think we do. Help us to grow together by the day-to-day assurance that we are not replacements for the loves of your lives, but that we ARE the loves of your lives…the newest chapters in your life stories…the best and most intriguing ones by far.

Faithfully yours,

Your Wives

Life Goes On—So Get A Grip!

In any second marriage, it's only natural to want better than the first wife had, and even more so as a WOW. If "her" greeting cards were full of mushy sentiments from your husband, then you expect and want YOUR cards to be mushier. If "she" got gifts of jewelry from him, you want him to adorn you with diamonds forever. And if he doesn't "stand and deliver", you take that to mean that he just doesn't love you as much as he did his late wife.

Along those same lines, if your husband insists on decorating the new Christmas tree with "her" unusual (read: tacky) ornaments alongside of yours, it's only natural to want to "accidentally" (read: purposefully) break them. If your husband is a grave-visitor, it's only natural for you to want to move to another city (or country!) to get as far away from her memorial as possible. And how many times must you hear her name before you can stop that facial tic from developing into a grimace?!

Then there's those infamous awkward moments, such as when you meet an acquaintance of your husband's who never knew his late wife, but assumes YOU are "she", followed by the discussion, once again, about how and when she died…and by the way, this is my "new" wife. Ugh!

You start to wonder if the past will ever really BE the past! In other words, you want to bury her all over again, and wipe her off the face of the earth—memories, family, belongings, and all—and go on with your marriage and your life, pretending she never existed at all! But then the Guilt Monster rears its ugly head and takes hold of your emotions, forcing you to stifle your feelings as soon as it wags its judgmental finger at you for being such a selfish, mean-spirited and self-centered woman.

As normal and natural as WOW feelings are, there are still some things about the late wife that you must learn to accept, and there are some things you can do to make it easier for both you and your husband:

1.) *Accept that she will NEVER go away completely.*

She was a vital human being, and left many loved ones and memories behind. That, you cannot take away. She will probably always be a part of your life, of your marriage, and of your husband's heart and memory, to some degree. Your husband cannot change the past, nor can you love him enough to make him forget it.

You can hide her pictures, redecorate her house, or refuse to utter her name ever again. But nothing will change the fact that you and the late wife will always be inextricably linked by your husband and/or his children, and by your marriage. While this sounds ominously depressing at first glance, the late wife never becomes any more of a threat to you than you allow her to be. The choice is always up to *you*.

When you come to accept that his late wife bears no real threat to your marriage, then it's easier to move to #2…

2.) *Learn to "share", but only after you have set the boundaries that you are comfortable with!*

Learn to incorporate his, "her", and "their" leftovers into your life and marriage, if you can. That includes her family, her belongings, and anything or anyone else she left behind. To do otherwise is to exclude from your husband's life what he has learned to hold dear before you came into it. He'll probably have no problem ridding the home of things that make you uncomfortable if you talk to your husband about your feelings, and figure out a way to make your marriage the priority while still allowing him his mementos. After all, they are merely token reminders of his past, and even though they are sentimental in nature, they pose no serious threat to your marriage. Family and friends must be shared, too, as they represent more than just a reminder of the late wife—they are symbols of your husband's capacity to love. They will learn to accept you much quicker if you can do the same for them.

If, after examining your shared items/people together, you still cannot possibly stand to look at the ornaments or deal with her family, and you get that awful, insecure feeling of what they represent every time you are faced with them, then by all means, talk to him about this, too, and allow him the opportunity to hear you out and work out a solution with you…together. A marriage based on the fear of your partner's reaction is not on solid ground to begin with. Build that firm foundation by facing the demons of your insecurity and allowing your husband the opportunity to deflect them by reassuring you.

3.) *Stand your ground and remind your husband to speak in the present tense.*

What I mean by this is that you have my permission to whack him upside the head if he ever refers to you in mixed company as "my second wife"! OK, I am not advocating violence, but there should be NO allusions to the past or to his late wife when referring to you. Neither should his late wife be referred to by your husband as "my wife" or "my first wife". "Late wife" is fine. Reminding him to speak in the present *tense* will ease his transition into his present *life* much quicker.

I remember a funeral I attended with my husband shortly after we were married. The embalmer recognized him from his late wife's funeral, and they stood with their backs to me, talking about that day. I overheard my husband refer to his late wife as "my wife" one too many times before I finally butted in and said, "Gee, Honey, I didn't know *I* was dead!" This is a great example of how NOT to solve the problem of "titles"! I should have been more respectful and certainly less rude! However, although I regret the embarrassment I caused my husband, an important boundary was set that day, and he has tried very hard ever since to speak in the present tense and never unintentionally hurt me like that again.

Marriage to a widower should be 75% present tense, 24% future tense, and 1% past tense. If the past was too perfect for him, the present is bound to be tense for both of you! That's another reason why it is vital to speak of the late wife with your husband. It "humanizes" her, and allows your husband insight into the reality of his present life.

4.) *Learn to "detach" and "reaffirm".*

What this means is simply this: when the times come where your husband may feel The Grief Monster yank on his heart (like when the past comes back to haunt him—and thereby, *you*—on her death anniversary, their wedding anniversary, etc.), and this gives way to insecurity in your heart, try some self-affirmation. Detach yourself from the situation, maintaining your understanding and sympathy without being consumed or involved personally. Talk calmly to yourself, reminding yourself that with time, his grief will subside more and more. Be gentle with yourself and remember that YOU are the present—the "here and now"—and you are alive while she is gone. Tell yourself over and over again that she is not a threat to you, but only a memory, and that your own memories with your husband are dearer to his heart than you think.

This advice may seem like an oversimplification for a heart-wrenchingly difficult situation, but believe me when I tell you that it works. Self-affirmation is actually training the brain to think positively. When we think positively, we act positively. When our positive thoughts and actions are in sync with each other, we effectively close the door to insecurity and self-doubt.

Sex And The WOW

Most wives of widowers with whom I communicated while doing research for the book told me that they secretly bury their issues on this subject of "Sex and The WOW", feeling so embarrassed and/or ashamed of their fears, insecurities, and feelings that they found it difficult to even discuss them with me under a cloak of anonymity!

WHAT a shock, especially in today's sexually enlightened society!

Shocking, yes—but understandable. As a happily married wife of a widower, I, too, have been loathe to personally discuss this topic for fear that I would be judged harshly, perhaps even thought of as a tad crazy. But the fact remains—existing in our society is a small segment of women who have battled or continue to battle things unseen…even in the bedroom.

When I met my previously widowed husband, his late wife had been deceased for close to three years. However, he still resided in the house they had shared together during their seven-year marriage, complete with all of their furniture, pictures adorning the walls, and even her coats hanging in the foyer closet. It looked as though she had just stepped out to the grocery store, not died prematurely a few years prior.

My first visit to his home was to be our first night of romance. However, I constantly felt "her" presence. The mementos of her that I faced during my visit were reminders that I was merely a guest and not "the lady of the house".

The most chilling remnant of her life was, of course, their bedroom. I doubt that my macho husband had chosen the pink and white lace bedspread and matching curtains after she had passed, so it was a reminder to me that this was at one time HER domain, causing me to feel like a trespasser and an adulteress. Needless to say, it was a tad intimidating to me as his new love interest.

The bed itself represented not only a place where they once laid their heads in rest, but also the shrine of intimacy where they once spoke of dreams, shared their feelings for each other, and yes…made passionate love. How could I possibly even think of coupling in such a way with him on the very same bed where *they* climbed the heights of passion and intertwined their souls as happily married people do?

With closet doors flung widely open, I could almost picture her in the neatly hung and pressed negligee's that draped their way casually from padded hangers there. It felt almost voyeuristic to me. Their wedding picture and wedding invitation were displayed in gilded frames that hung in all their glory over the bed, as if to speak for her: "Remember where you are and whom you are with? I knew him better and longer than you!" Of course, this was not the picture-perfect, romantic evening that I had dreamed of! *Too many ghosts.*

Her belongings, which produced images of her, were not the only windmills at which I tilted. There was also the issue of *comparison*. How would I measure up—sexually speaking—to a woman who knew my then-boyfriend so intimately? Considering the fact that they dated for a year before marrying, they collectively shared 8 years of a loving relationship. This gave them plenty of time to figure out how to please each other, to chart the roadmaps of each other's bodies, and to communicate to each other their deepest romantic desires. Foreplay would have been set in stone, each knowing what turned the other on, and the dance of sexual passion would have been played out in satisfying synchronization.

Gulp! What a tough act to follow!

Of course, making love for the first time with a new love interest is always nerve provoking. But as a new lover of a former widower, I had an eerie feeling that "she" was watching us, as if to make sure that I would not best her in the sexual arena. Add to that mixture an almost omnipresent feeling—one that nudges your competitive nature and makes you feel that you and your lover are *not* the only two people in the bed—and you have a recipe for intimidation and thoughts of failure before you even begin to take your clothes off!

When the lights were dimmed and our passion sparked, I almost forgot about "her"...until I turned my head to face my sweetheart, and found his eyes closed. I wondered if he was thinking of "her". With every one of his touches, I insecurely thought that he might have been imagining my body as her body. I started to doubt his whispered words of love for me, and felt that he was probably pretending to say them to her. I had wondered if all the grief information I had read was true—that perhaps he may have had feelings of guilt for "betraying" his late wife's memory. I was filled with confusion…and anger, since I was not the kind of person who would be willing to share my man with another woman.

Bolting from the bedroom, I suppose my sweetie thought I was insane. But we had shared enough time together in our dating history to forge a firm foundation of trust in our relationship, so I finally blurted out the truth about my fears and anxieties. It was the beginning of a new understanding…and a new life of sexual fulfillment for us.

Eventually, her closet's contents were donated to charity and the wedding pictures stored away for safekeeping. Their bed was sold, as was their house, and we bought our own home and purchased our own bed. But until that time, we had sweet, romantic trysts in hotel rooms and other rooms of the house where the late wife's presence was not so overpowering for me, and we made our own beautiful sexual memories together, away from "her" watchful eye.

With gentle reassurance, my husband guided me out of my fears and convinced me that he had never compared my sexual prowess to his late wife's. He confirmed to me that I was a wonderful lover, partner, and friend, so I began to feel more secure about myself and about our relationship. After a time, the threat of the late wife's memory ceased to exist, and no longer haunted me or forced me to "out-do" her in the bedroom.

The pink and white lace bedspread was burned in effigy, and a royal-colored floral comforter now graces the mattresses where my husband and I renew our intertwined spirits with passion and speak of our future plans. This is now MY domain, and I am now "the lady of THIS house", relegating the late wife to the role of the outsider…a stranger whom I accept my husband will always love, and one who will often trip into my thoughts, but one who no longer trespasses on our lives in our bedroom.

Home Sweet Home

When my previously widowed husband and I started dating seriously, we naturally spent time in each other's homes. Having been previously divorced, my home was "clean", meaning that my ex-husband had already laid claim to his possessions and taken them with him to his new home. The remaining mementos and pictures that I had kept for my children's future enjoyment were carefully stored in locked, airtight containers in my attic, so the house my ex-husband and I had once owned together now had no signs of his ever having lived there by the time my new husband came into my life.

However, my now-husband's home was still amazingly chock full of his late wife's things, even after almost three years. Her pictures still adorned his walls; ticket stubs to events they had attended together tucked neatly inside a frame here and there; her hope chest with its sentimental contents still sitting at the foot of their bed; and even her coats and clothes still hanging neatly in her closet. It looked as if she had never left, much less forever. In fact, my husband's home looked as if his late wife had just stepped out momentarily to the store, and would be coming home soon.

And I suppose that is why they were still there. I believe that my husband was in some kind of grief stage, like denial, at the time—feeling that the removal of her belongings would mean he had to accept her loss once and for all. He wanted to move ahead with his life and open his heart to me, but he wasn't sure how to begin. He was sort of "stuck" in a necessary transition, but it was enough for me that he even wanted to learn how to deal with this issue, so I was hopeful.

Everyone views another person's belongings differently. To some, they are representations of the owners themselves, perhaps reflecting a moment in time that was cherished, or a glimpse into the owner's personality. To others, they are mere objects with no significant meaning attached, signifying nothing more than the owner's desire to possess them.

I am the former. Everything I own has sentimental value, if not purpose. For instance, my bedspread is not just a comforter, but also the wrap of two inter-twined souls who share more than a bed. My pictures are of images long past, but still near and dear to my memory. And like a detective hot on the trail, I look at other people's possessions as a challenge to discovering their inner selves, as if they've whispered a secret to me.

Needless to say, knowing this about myself, I found it very uncomfortable to be situated in full view of the late wife's things, feeling that *their* presence equaled *her* presence. But I was also unnerved because I felt their purpose had died along with her, so there was no reason in my mind why these things shouldn't be stored, thrown away, donated to charity, or given to her family. My husband, however, had a different view.

He had a hard time letting go of her things because they were as sentimental to him as they had been to her. Alas, I discovered that my husband was like me, giving intrinsic heart-felt value to every article. I compared my packed-away, post-divorce possessions, trying to make the point that the past was the past, and I no longer had warm and fuzzy feelings for my ex husband nor his things, so why put them on display? He countered, saying that he and his wife did not part on bad terms, so the sentimentality attached to the items was still there. At that moment, I wanted to chuck all of her things into a bonfire and light the match with glee! But, I reminded myself that my husband's feelings mattered, too. Was there a compromise to be had that would consider both of our feelings? Fortunately, yes.

After much discussion, we decided together that with the help of his family, we would donate the clothing to charity, give the late wife's jewelry to her family, and pack the mementos and pictures in a nice steamer trunk which, I agreed, my husband could "visit" in the basement now and then when he felt the need.

I believe that truly living in the present doesn't necessarily mean that one must forget about the past, but to work through the memories of it until one can come to a place in the present where mere possessions and reminders of the past do not effect one's life negatively. Knowing my husband was now at that place in his life, this compromise worked for him, for me, and for us.

Would the compromise work for all WOWs? Actually, I know of a few WOWs who do not consider the "possessions issue" a problem, and are more than comfortable with having the late wife's things intermixed with their own, even allowing the late wife's picture to sit on the fireplace mantle. One WOW I know tells me that she passes the photograph daily and even whispers a "thank you" to the late wife's image, as if to remind herself to be grateful for her husband and how the late wife had contributed to making him the person she loves. What a wonderful way to look at this whole issue! But we can't all be that generous of spirit while we struggle with our WOW issues.

Every new bride wants her home to be a reflection of her taste, style, and personality, and also of the life and love she shares with her new husband. Anyone else's possessions feel like an intrusion of sorts. For the WOW, it appears to be vital that she make a new home with her previously widowed husband that reflects only their present life together, without any remnants of a past life in full view. To be forced to live in the same home where the late wife had once lived, loved, and shared with her husband apparently makes the WOW feel as if she isn't really "home" at all, but just a guest in another woman's house.

Therefore, most new WOWs feel that their husbands' desire to keep the late wives' things and live in the same house he had shared with her represents a threat to the sanctity of their present marital unions. We just cannot feel comfortable with having the late wives' possessions around, serving as a nudge to our WOW insecurities, nor can we tolerate feeling like an intruder in another woman's home…and that's OK, too. As long as both the husbands and the wives are sensitive to each other's needs and feelings, open communication will bring about a change that will be satisfactory to all.

I Know Why The Caged WOW Sings

Trying to interpret poetry is, to me, like trying to work a Rubik's cube. It looks fascinating until you get your hands on it, then all frustration breaks loose. Yet you just can't seem to put it down until you have unraveled the mystery.

So it was when I first encountered, "I Know Why The Caged Bird Sings". While struggling to comprehend what the author had in mind when he wrote this beautiful prose, I acquired my own assortment of theories about the meaning of caged birds blissfully tweeting away, though imprisoned for their lifetimes.

I like poetry that reflects life and the average man, so I put my OWN shoes on…those WOW (Wife Of a Widower) moccasins…and again reread this philosophical mind-bender. Although I may never fully understand poetry, especially this particular poem, it did make me think about the uneasy, restless hearts that beat within all WOWs—the ones that yearn to be free from the past.

Here's what I surmised:

Perhaps a caged bird will sing because it is his inherent nature. After all, he has no idea that to mourn his loss of freedom means to stop singing. Like birds, we humans are born free, live free, and die free. At least that's the way it's supposed to be. But what is freedom? Sure, it is the right of all individuals to pursue happiness. But how can you be truly happy if you have walls around you…or around your heart? Doesn't the definition of freedom also include the right to be free from the chains the bind you…perhaps those of your past…or of your husband's past…or of the ghosts from the past that invade your present life?

On the other hand, perhaps Tweety's heart is merry just because he is merely alive, so he sings in gleeful whistles to announce his joie de vivre. Perhaps he just doesn't know any better. But what about the QUALITY of his life? Wouldn't we rather he not sing but screech in protest of the clipped-winged life he now endures? Would we not rage at those who would cage us…imprison our very souls…just for their own personal satisfaction and amusement? Would we WOWs not rant in defiance if our husbands refused to share intimately with us about his grief, his pain, and his past, just because he doesn't want to talk about it or "burden" us with it? Isn't silence just as deafening as speech…and just as monumental in the walls it builds?

But I digress…I mean, who are we to impose our own morality or sanctions on another's definition of freedom? Maybe, just maybe, a caged bird is just plain happy to be safe in a home that protects him from the fears, insanity, and ravages of the real world. Maybe, just maybe, a WOW is better off not knowing about her husband's prior life or former wife. After all, ignorance IS bliss…or is it? Doesn't working *through* your fears first mean *knowing* your "enemy" intimately, facing the fears "she" imposes, and *fighting* them for a glimpse at the light we know is at the end of the dark tunnel, until we emerge victorious in the afterglow of our renewed strength and redefined attitude? Isn't that what real freedom is?

To all those WOWs who tilt at the silent windmills of your minds…Can you honestly say that you are happy being married to a man who suffers in silence, not sharing his heart with you about something so meaningful, so huge, so life-altering…and denying you the opportunity—nay, the need—to purge the overblown anxieties you have built in your own mind out of fear of the unknown?

I know why the caged WOW sings, but more importantly, I know *when*. She sings when she is finally free from the insecurities and jealousies that plague her—those fears that had taken on a life of their own because of the lack of the necessary knowledge about the past required to release them.

She may, like the caged bird, be forever surrounded by the iron bars of the late wife's ever-present memory. But when within her very soul she is unchained from the self-imposed threat of the late wife's existence in her husband's heart, by facing the demons of self-doubt and casting them out one by one, the WOW will warble triumphantly for the sweet victory that comes from accepting things that cannot be changed, finding happiness in spite of them, and discovering that life is worth singing about when you are free unto yourself and within your own heart.

4

HOLIDAYS AND OTHER "GRIEF TRIGGERS"

As I mentioned before, there will be times in your marriage when your husband's grief will be stronger than others, and it usually happens on special occasions such as the anniversary of his late wife's death, her birthday, their wedding anniversary, and holidays. And while you want to become understanding and sympathetic, you also worry that these occasions of grief will somehow put a chink in the armor of your marriage. Fear not—for these "grief triggers" are only temporary and, believe it or not, *necessary* to the healing of grief.

The following are a few of my personal stories of special "grief triggers" from my marriage:

The Ghost of Christmas Past

Every new bride dreams of the first Christmas she will share with her new husband. She wants it to be perfect, special, and wonderful. She conjures up images of snow gently falling in the moonlight upon the earth below, while a fire roars in the fireplace, as her new husband and she merrily decorate their freshly cut Christmas tree with ornaments they have purchased together or been given in their honor, each one with a heartfelt meaning attached. They gaze lovingly into each other's eyes, knowing this is a unique occasion that has never been and will never be repeated. Their minds are focused only on the other, and how blessed they are to have found one another.

We WOWs also want a special holiday that will burn into our memory for years to come, too. And while we can have all these special moments, there are a few glaring exceptions and challenges, with the biggest issue being dealing with the Ghost of Christmas Past (or in other words, the late wife).

My First Christmas Experience

The first Christmas season my widowed husband and I shared together early in our relationship was a turning point in his grief journey. I recall floodgates of tears as the "Ghost" made her appearance in the form of "their" significant mementos and unabashed memory sharing. He was nearing his third year of grief, and had not had a significant other with whom to share his holidays since her death. As each of "their" ornaments made its way out of the storage box and onto his tree, my husband regaled me with story after story of "their" Christmases and what each bauble meant to him and to her.

While I truly wanted to be the supportive and sympathetic partner, my heart was breaking. It seemed as if there was nothing special left for us to share that would be wonderful in his eyes, since he had already shared it all with "her". Selfishly, I felt as if my presence meant nothing to him, and I began to wonder why I was even there, trying to revive his otherwise dismal holiday spirit. *Would all our holidays be like this—full of only "her" memories and his sadness?* I worried. But I persevered; hoping once we got passed the decorating, things would improve. No such luck.

On that Christmas morning, I eagerly sat next to him on "their" couch, in "their" house, in front of "their" artificial tree, with "their" Christmas CDs playing in the background, secretly hoping that my gift from him would be so thoughtful and so beautiful that my insecurities would be washed clean and replaced by wonderful new traditions and memories of our own. Imagine my shock and disappointment to open my gift and find a pair of flannel pajamas with a snapped drop-bottom in the rear! Unromantic, to say the least. But a bigger disappointment than that was knowing, beforehand, that the late wife's first gift from him was an opal ring with diamonds and a greeting card that dripped with sentimentality and hopes of their future together—and I got a union suit!!

This was not the one-of-a-kind piece of jewelry that signifies a man's deep desire to make his woman happy. This was not the sentimental, "I know her so well" gift that every woman dreams of receiving from the man she loves.

Oh no! This gift didn't even come with a lousy greeting card! THIS, my friends, was a gift that said, "I'm still not sure of my feelings for you, and I'm still so deep in grief that I'm not so sure I'll ever be sure". The Ghost of Christmas Past had done what she came to do…and I wanted to hate her for it.

The Ghost Of Christmas Present

Dinner that evening was to be enjoyed at the Ghost of Christmas Present's house, also known as my mother-in-law—a kindly widow of age 69 who welcomed me, loved me as if I were her own child, and was happy I had come into the family fold, but even more so into her son's life. This was a woman, although sweet and petite, to be reckoned with, for she took no prisoners, even her own children, when she was crossed. Tonight was to be no exception. Having noticed her son's gloomy behavior all through dinner and throughout the evening, I discovered years later that this wise and wonderful lady, while I packed the car with our gifts, took her son aside and sternly spoke a reasonable facsimile of these words, with a mother's love and a widow's heart:

> *"Holidays have always been a little hard for me since your father passed away, son. But you'd never know it, would you? You only see me smiling and enjoying my family. That's because what happens on each Christmas day is more joyful, more wonderful, more special, and bigger, than the grief I bear. And do you know why? Because life is for the living—and I'm not through living mine yet! And YOU, my dear son, need to remember that you have just begun to live yours. I have so many children to love and grandchildren to watch grow. My past is bright with memories, and my future will be, too, as long as I remember that TODAY is my gift—the most precious gift of all—and the people you love and who love you today are what makes Christmas wonderful."*

Make It Your OWN!

I believe that every day of life is a gift from God, and to live for the present is to show your appreciation for such a gift. Those who live life to the fullest and embrace with love the special people around them for the joy that they bring will never grieve so badly that the Ghost of Christmas Past ruins their holidays. They will laugh, love, share, and be happy, even if the Ghost makes an occasional appearance.

I wish I could say that from that day forward, I received from my husband the best sentiments that Hallmark™ had to offer, jewelry to adorn a queen, and never again had to face the Ghost of Christmas Past. But, I CAN tell you that I have always received flannel pajamas each Christmas, because they represent a special, funny tradition, unique to my marriage and no one else's...and I couldn't be merrier.

I now experience Christmas as it should be for every married couple: snow gently falling in the moonlight upon the earth below while a fire roars in the hearth, as my husband and I merrily decorate our freshly cut Christmas tree with ornaments we have purchased together or been given in our honor, each one with a heartfelt meaning attached. We celebrate life in "our" home, open gifts on "our" couch, with "our" CDs playing in the background. We gaze lovingly into each other's eyes, knowing this is a unique occasion that has never been and will never be repeated. Our minds are focused only on the other, and on how blessed we are to have found one another.

God bless us...everyone.

New Year Resolutions for WOWs

What ARE resolutions anyway? They are promises we make to ourselves in earnest, usually having something to do with self-improvement. But we are human, and try as we may, there will be times when our resolve is weak, and we teeter on the brink of failure. This may compel us to give up altogether, but we must certainly NEVER give up trying to come to grips with our WOW fears, or else we stand to lose so much happiness for our futures.

I have always regarded New Year's as a new lease on life or a new beginning. It's a second chance to make amends, to forgive myself and others, and to try harder. It has always felt like a breaking of the chains that bound me; a "soul-cleansing", if you will. I whisper them like a prayer, but words without actions are useless, so I try to accomplish them in small steps.

In the past, as Dec. 31st approached, I would make a list of my "WOW New Year's Resolutions". I would work diligently at keeping them, but then promptly fail by at least the end of February. Still, every New Year's Eve, I resolve to renew my resolutions, regardless of my aptitude for failure. Why? Because I think just taking a positive step towards better mental health, no matter how small, is worth the effort. And it seems to be working. I am feeling much more secure in my marriage, and stronger in my resolve, with each passing year.

So, to start, I resolve first and foremost to forgive myself should I temporarily fail to keep my resolutions. After all, tomorrow is another day…and another new year is just around the corner.

The following are 20 New Year's Resolutions for WOWs. I hope they will encourage you to make a positive effort to overcome WOW anxiety for the coming year.

I RESOLVE TO:

…stop comparing myself unfavorably to the late wife.

…believe my husband when he tells me I am beautiful, sexy, and attractive, etc.—without feeling that he is comparing me to his late wife.

…react with more sympathy and selflessness when those "dates" come (i.e., death anniversary, their wedding anniversary, etc.).

…make holidays special just for he and I, and try not to allow the "Ghost of Holidays Past" to ruin my happiness.

…make vacation plans well in advance so we can build our cache of memories.

…remind myself to live in the "here and now" and not in the past.

…celebrate our special occasions with gusto to show the significance of my husband in my life.

…stop demanding so much of my husband's love to prove that he loves me more than "her", and start appreciating all that he has to offer to me.

…soothe myself with daily affirmations and prayer, knowing that I am worthy of my husband's love.

…restore hope in my heart and in my marriage by making a concerted effort every day to overcome my WOW anxieties.

…do more practical things to keep from exhausting today's energies with tomorrow's problems.

…accept the things I cannot change, and change the things I am able to.

…banish worry from my mind and live for the moment.

…not allow circumstances to rule my life, but bring forth change with a new attitude.

…not allow anything, even the late wife or his memories of her, to separate me from my joy.

…be more open and honest about my WOW insecurities with my husband, and not be afraid to discuss them with him.

…take control of how my WOW issues affect my moods.

…realize that I can release this WOW burden up to a higher power whenever I need a moment of peace, remembering that I am not alone.

…make peace with "their" past.

…embrace the late wife within the boundaries that define my comfort zone.

5

EMBRACING THE LATE WIFE

In the beginning of our relationship, my husband actually felt comfortable telling me about his late wife. There was an aura of mystery about her, mostly because I had not known her prior to her death. To sate my curiosity, I just wanted to know the answers to a few basic questions, and my husband was more than willing to oblige me. We were still in that "getting to know you" stage of newfound love, so he had nothing to lose by sharing some basic background information with me about her—the "non-intimate details" of his late wife, such as where she attended school, what job she held prior to her death, the cause of her death, etc.

So, for that time being, I was satisfied with just knowing the basics. Soon after marrying him, however, knowing more about her became an addiction that needed satisfying and a hunger to be sated.

The Obsession to Know Her

I remember exactly when the obsession took shape. During the first week of our marriage, I found a folder in his old filing cabinet, and in it were signed papers for an adoption process. Apparently, unbeknownst to me, he and his late wife had actually attempted to become the adoptive parents of a child. I looked at the date, and was saddened to see that the papers were filed in between the time she discovered she had cancer and her actual death.

Perhaps this meant that she regretted not having any biological children of her own with him, and now wanted to share parenthood with him before she passed away, leaving a legacy of herself behind.

Whatever her reasons, I was taken aback. Previously, my husband's late wife had been, in my naïve mind, just another woman from his past. Prior to this discovery, I had only received a simple biography or factual resume of her life—nothing to substantiate anything more meaningful or intimate. But now, with this new information, she became much more than that.

It was as if I had been in denial—an "ignorance is bliss" sort of reasoning—since the beginning. But now, all at once, I looked upon her with my heart instead of only my mind. And the realization hit me like a ton of bricks—she was, at one time, a living, breathing, valuable human being. She was a woman, with emotions, needs, and desires, just like me. *And this real person was one flesh with my husband!* In one split second, she went from a sheet of useless data to a real person, and I wanted to know her…intimately.

It's been said that the best way to defeat an enemy is to know him, or in this case, her. And at that time, I suddenly felt more threatened by her than I had ever felt by anyone else in my life. She became, in my mind, "the other woman". She had not only shared a past with my husband, but a bed, a home, a life, her dreams, her body, and eventually, her illness and death. That made her special, beloved, and unique…*especially to him.*

Ugh! I had never really thought about it that way before! She was so much easier for me to deal with when I thought of her as a one-dimensional non-entity with non-specific details to describe her non-life! Sure, there were enough pictures of her to validate that she did at one time walk this earth and fill space…but now, I had to swallow the painful truth that she did more than that.

So, with my obsession pumping me with energy, I went straight to the source—my husband—armed with enough intimate questions as my arsenal to slay the beast that threatened the security and priority I had always thought I held in my husband's heart. It must have been the fire in my eyes as I pummeled him with my ammo—questions—that made him put up his shield, but he closed up tight, built a wall, and refused to play my game.

He would not share with me her faults! He would not paint a picture for me of their day-to-day life as man and wife! He would not regale me with amusing anecdotes of her personality! He refused to succumb to my ploy to bleed him dry of information pertaining to what made her special, what made her real, what made her…loved by *him.*

Oh my God, I anguished, *It's worse than I thought! This evasion was proof—he loved her more than he loved me! He thinks she was perfect! And he's holding her up on some unattainable pedestal, where she will forever sit, canonized and sainted by him, every day of his life!* I will never be *Number One* in his heart!

Fighting A Losing Battle With Fear

I thought my marriage was doomed. How could I share his heart with another woman? And how could he want to marry me in the first place if I meant less than she did to him?

For a year, I managed to depressingly drag my way through my marriage, day after day, while still holding onto the anger and hating his late wife more and more. I used up so much energy doing this that I was exhausted all the time. My self-esteem plummeted. I dreaded his touch, for fear he was thinking in comparisons…"My late wife was much softer"…"My late wife was a much better lover"…"My late wife…" etc., ad nauseum.

I just couldn't take it any more, and seriously considered divorce as the only alternative, since there was no way I was going to spend the rest of my life with a man who split his love between me and a ghost. But leaving him would mean she had *won,* and I wasn't about to let her take him from me completely! There had to be a better way! I wanted validation of my fears and feelings.

Finally, I arranged for a session with a psychologist who was also a grief counselor. After sobbing my story to him, he asked me if I would do a simple exercise: write a letter to the late wife as if she could read it herself. I came very close to quitting therapy and forever labeling my therapist as the world's biggest quack before I finally gave this idea a chance.

"Dear Late Wife…"

A week later, with pen and paper in hand, I drove to the cemetery and sat by the late wife's marker while I poured out my heart. Amazingly, though, once I started writing to her as if she were sitting right next to me, a funny thing happened. My anger faded away, and was replaced by sorrowful compassion. It was as if something—or someone—was guiding my hand. This is what I wrote:

"I wish I could meet you. I would like to have known the kind of woman my husband chose the first time around…and why. I'd like to think that because of our mutual love for him, we might have been good friends. We probably have more in common than we do not."

"And oh, I would have had so many questions to ask you! What strengths and fears do we share? What was it about our husband that first attracted you? What was it about him that you loved so much? How did he propose to you? How was your sex life? Too personal? Sorry, but it does cross my mind, especially when his eyes are closed during our lovemaking".

"Do you know how guilty I feel sometimes, just knowing that I am here only because you are not—that I am living the life that you could have lived had you not died? Your death also left so many fears for me…will I ever be #1 in my husband's heart? Will I always live in your shadow? Will your memory and the ghost of you always be in the back of his heart, overshadowing anything good he may feel for me? Will he always hold you up so high on that damned pedestal that I can't get near it? Do you know how much I envy you? You were the "first", and nothing will ever change that. I will always be just the "second", even though I am happy to be a part of his heart at all."

"I know this all sounds selfish. You didn't ASK to die, and you didn't want to, either. I know our husband wishes he could have spared you the excruciating pain you endured with cancer. I'm so sorry that you were too young to die. You had so much more life ahead of you, so much more love to share. He loved you so."

"But since you did die, he had to move on. I hope you don't hold that against him. Could you please let him go…release that hold on him that grips his heart with sadness sometimes? I'm sure that if you loved him as you did, you would want him to be happy".

"And he is happy, really. We have a baby now. Did you get to hold her in Heaven before she was born? She is the perfect image of him, so I know you felt a

part of our husband when you kissed her sweet face. I want that to be a nice memory for you. I'm sorry you didn't have children. Our husband is such a great daddy, and for him, the sun rises and sets on his daughter. I know you would want that for him."

"Thank you for helping to make him who he is today, the man I love and adore. I know you had something to do with that in the short time you had together. Perhaps, when you see him again, he will be even that much better a person than the one you left behind. I hope that will help you forgive me."

Cleansing My Soul

When I had finished, I felt relieved. The burden of all the rage I had felt was instantaneously lifted from my shoulders. I cried for hours. It was as if I had been grieving her loss myself. I felt almost a sisterhood with her, and started to feel guilty about having hated her. I didn't hate her. I hated me. But now, I loved us both.

When my next session with the psychologist came, I gave the letter to him to read. This wise, wonderful advisor looked at me with sympathetic eyes, and asked, "So, how does it feel to have forgiven *yourself?*"

Myself? Hmm…I hadn't thought of it that way. But he was right. Instead of forgiving the late wife for all the things I had accused her of and all the things I had conjured up in my insecure mind, I came to accept that since she was the innocent party, it was *me* who needed forgiveness, and only I could grant it.

Consciously, I knew that the insecurities I had plagued myself with were based on hypothetical and illogical reasoning. But subconsciously, I couldn't help it. I wanted someone to blame for making me feel so insecure. I blamed her, when I really should have taken more responsibility for my negative feelings in the first place.

I suppose I will always wonder about the life my husband shared with his late wife, and I'm sure I will always be curious about the person she was. It's no longer an obsession that lives to spite her, but more of a quiet reflection of a woman who shares my husband's heart. It has taken time, but since I have become the master of my own feelings about the past and made my peace with it

(AND with the late wife), my life with and marriage to a widower has become much easier.

Embracing the late wife is relatively easy if you can humbly give credit where credit is due, since the late wife was a perfectly valuable person, worthy of love and compassion. Forgiving yourself is the first step in healing the guilt you may bear for having blamed her for feeling rage or hatred.

The next step is to remember that, even if you never hear a disparaging word about her, the late wife was not a saint. The seemingly flawless windmills you tilt at are only those in your mind. Embracing her only means accepting her for who and what she was, faults and all, including what she gave to your husband. But most of all, embracing the late wife means accepting that you two will be forever linked not by jealousy or a sense of competition but by the love you both share(d) with your husband.

Mama Never Said There'd Be Days Like These!

(Author's note: *The following is an article I had printed on several online web-sites, and received hundreds of pleasant responses from widows, widowers, and WOWs from all over the world. Love is universal, and is would appear that people worldwide can relate to love's healing power and the light it shines when times are at their dark-est. I hope you can, too.*)

My mother was the wisest person I ever knew. I still recall endless hours of intently listening to her fascinating life stories and pearls of wisdom, even as we worked together at some mundane chore like folding the family laundry. The ease at which she delivered to me her lessons of life always made me feel confident that there would never be an obstacle in my life that would be too high to hurdle. Armed with the arsenal of Mom's sage advice, I knew there would never be a rag-ing river too wild for me to cross, nor any mountain too high for me to climb.

Mom never said that life would always be smooth—she only offered a reverent belief that nothing was impossible if you just believed in yourself and held tight to the power of love. In essence, my mother's affirmation that "nothing was impossible with love to guide you" gave me hope for my future.

Mom had married my father, her high school sweetheart—someone she had known since she was 6 years old. They remained happily married for 50 odd years. She had never been forced to contend with the heartbreak of divorce or the puzzlement of remarriage. That journey was mine alone. But Mom's loving instruction was like a fine chain that linked one generation to the next. It has always flowed freely within my heart like a gently rolling river, whose reservoirs I have tapped countless times in my life's journey when I have encountered a thirst for wisdom along my life's journey.

However, being the wife of a widower, I have encountered days for which my mother never prepared me—anniversaries wracked with grief and emotion, such as that one day each year which marks the day my husband's late wife died.

To be sure, Mom never said there'd be days like these!

After all, no one has ever written a step-by-step instruction manual that teaches wives of widowers how to prepare their hearts for these moments, and there is a shortage of people who can relate to the depth and variety of emotions that flood these days. Therefore, we who walk in these WOW shoes must rely on the strength that has been molded inside our genetic composition from our mother's wisdom—along with the perseverance that has guided us through life thus far. On days like these, we must again tap into that source of courage that enables us to endure, knowing all along that there is a light at the end of every dark tunnel.

That source, and that light, is *love*.

As I write this, I am reminded that tomorrow, my husband's late wife—the love of his youth—will have been gone for exactly 6 years. This rather sad and unceremonious day is never easy for my husband or for myself, for it is not a day of celebration as a birthday would be, nor is it a day that should be ignored, either. So again, I must draw upon the wisdom of my heritage to guide me through it. I can almost hear my mother's kind voice, reminding me that "You can be better or bitter—the choice is up to YOU whether to change a situation, or just accept it and make the best of it!"

As my mother would have approved, I choose to look positively upon this dark day as a time to reflect on the people in my life who have deeply touched me and affected me by their love—either directly or indirectly.

It is not my choice to share my husband's heart with another woman, but it is something I have learned to accept. Part of that acceptance is recognizing that his late wife, because of her love for him, has contributed greatly to my husband's life and helped to forge his beautiful character, as all wives do. And because of this, she has indirectly touched *my* soul as well, since it is intertwined with the husband we share through our marriage.

As we hold hands together at the cemetery tomorrow and lay a rose at the base of the memorial that marks the late wife's grave, my husband and I will each whisper our own prayers based on our own personal feelings. My husband's prayer will most certainly be laced with regrets and sadness, and I will do my best to be a silent comfort to him as I vainly attempt to understand a grief that I know I will never fully comprehend.

My own graveside prayer will be one of thanks…gratitude for the women in my life who have sweetly branded my heart with their kind, loving, and generous spirits just by once existing on this earth—my husband's late wife, and my mother.

Their legacies of love will never be forgotten.

6

WOW AND THE "GUILT MONSTER"

The Story of "Carol"

It never really occurred to me that I might be "living another woman's life" until it was pointed out to me one day by a mutual friend of my husband's and his late wife's named "Carol". Hoping to cement a friendship that had started a year earlier, I invited her over for tea one snowy, lazy winter Saturday.

I was thrilled with my perception that the late wife's friends had accepted me so readily and so easily into the circle that had once included the late wife. But on that blustery December day, I noticed Carol hadn't touched her tea the whole time we had been chatting.

"But you LOVE chamomile!" I smiled. Nervously, Carol responded, "Yes, I do. But I'd rather not drink it out of the china tea cups that I gave "T" (my husband's late wife) the last Christmas of her life". Confused, I asked, "Whatever do you mean, Carol?"

Carol then proceeded to tell me that although she had come to accept me, even love me as a friend, she still had a hard time accepting that "T" was gone, and here *I* was, her "replacement".

"I'm sorry", she continued sadly, "but it's like you're living the life that "T" would be living if she were still alive, and a part of me irrationally resents that…and you".

May The Circle Be Unbroken

The sympathetic "me" wanted to throw my arms around an otherwise grief-stricken friend and comfort her, but the defensive WOW in me wanted to dump her tea over her head! I tried to understand what she had told me in a compassionate way, thinking that perhaps she was still walking her own grief journey, and I had naively thought that the late wife's friends must *surely* be beyond bereavement by now.

I felt so guilty about having ignored Carol's need for time (and my understanding) to come to grips with her friend's death, her friend's husband's grief, and his obvious moving on with his life by marrying me. I compassionately allowed that it must have been hard for the late wife's friends to see another woman (namely, me!) making her widowed husband so happy, or using her special china tea service, or just being alive and living in her stead. After all, they, the circle of friends, had no choice in the matter of who my husband would marry, and had no say as to his eventual choice. I was simply just thrust upon them one day, and they were forced to accept me.

There wasn't much more I could say to Carol at that time, but that afternoon, her comments had moved "The Guilt Monster" into my heart.

The "Guilt Monster" Must Die!

Do WOWs really "live another woman's life", that of the late wife, as Carol had determined? Or is it merely an innocently misguided perception from an "outsider's" point of view?

For one, my friend's observation had made me feel that if perhaps the outside world views all WOWs as their husbands' replacement of his late wife and nothing more, then this makes him sound too ill-equipped to make any reasonable decisions because of his loss, and reduces the WOW to a mere shadow of the late wife, with nothing more to offer. And God forbid if the two women actually resemble each other, have the same laugh, drive the same make and model of car, or use the same china tea service! My goodness, people must think that widowers only want to marry their late wives' exact replicas, or that their new wives have no distinct personality to call their own!

Also, another thing that really bothered me was how guilty I felt about the late wife and her life, or lack thereof. Hard as it is for us WOWs to swallow, the fact is, if the late wife had not died, our husbands would probably still be married to "her", living their daily lives merrily from one day to the next, doing the things husbands and wives do. The late wives did not choose to die. In a way, their lives and marriages were "stolen" from them without their consent, which leads many people to believe that she never gave her permission for her husband's remarriage, either. However, this does not make WOWs the husband-thieving bandits!! Just as late wives had no control over their own deaths, WOWs also had no hand in their demise, either, or for that matter, in the eventual rebuilding of the late wives' husbands' lives. These men had been doing that on their own, step by agonizing step, long before we WOWs came into the picture.

Although the "guilt monster" reared its ugly head and tried to trivialize the deep and loving commitment that I had found with my widowed husband in the days following my tea with Carol, in the end, I refused to allow the monster to shake me down. I had nothing to feel guilty about. This was now *my* life, *my* marriage…not the late wife's!

Sure, her life insurance policy was enough to buy the house that my husband and I purchased together, and I have sort of "inherited" many of her personal but trivial effects, such as the china tea service. Therefore, I am sure that by all appearances, it looks as if I have benefited somewhat from her demise. But in an odd way, so has my husband, since he is now a stronger, more resilient, more appreciative man because of having survived her death and rising from the ashes of grief.

Should he be made to feel guilty about that? I think not.

Oh, Give Me A Clone…

Granted, my husband's late wife and I share many common interests, such as camping, which might lead someone to believe that I am trying to replicate her life in order to please my husband. But nothing could be further from the truth, since there are also many thing I enjoy doing with him that she did not, and vice versa. Perhaps she and I also share many of the same tastes as well, since I have no problem using her cherished tea service as my own today. But I also have an antique silver tea set, a family heirloom, which graces my home, too. I rather enjoy my individuality, and I know my husband appreciates it as well.

The bottom line is this: The late wife and the WOW are two separate and entirely unique individuals, so how could they possibly lead parallel lives? And although the WOW may share with the late wife certain things in common, such as personality traits, hobbies, or personal tastes, this does not mean that her husband has chosen his new bride as a replacement or carbon copy. It just means that he has chosen a new life partner whom he enjoys—one who brings a new dimension to his life because she is unique and special in her own right.

Perhaps Carol will some day choose to accept me—all of me—as the person I am and not compare me to the person she misses. In the meantime, I'll just continue to be her friend and to be myself. Who *else* COULD I be?

Another Woman's Shadow

Still, once in a blue moon, I am asked, "What does it feel like to live in another woman's shadow?" Excuse me? Have I missed something here? It had never occurred to me that I am considered by some to be my husband's late wife's replacement until I was asked this question early in my marriage. Back then, the inquiry did throw me for a loop, if only for a moment.

As a "WOW", I sometimes have my resolve tested by the nosy inquiries of the ignorant few, but this one still gets on my nerves even today. It is a question more often than not that is posed by those who knew my husband's late wife. There are undertones of disapproval laced within this inquiry. Therefore, it is more of a judgment than a question. And I resent the brazen cover-up of spineless finger pointing just because the statement is made in the form of a question, as if the person doing the asking really cares what or how I feel! It is a gutless question that does more telling than asking, for I can read between its lines: The real purpose in asking this question is to inform the WOW that the person inquiring has made his/her judgment, and the WOW is somehow lacking in the questioner's comparison to the late wife.

So, in the spirit of educating those most cunning and lacking of spinal fluid, allow me to dissect this question and, once and for all, put it to rest.

Dear Questioner,

How can I "feel" anything about "living in another woman's shadow" when that is such an absurd observation to make? It conjures up images of some poor WOW desperately trying to BE the late wife, but failing. I no more wish to be the late wife than I wish to be the Queen of England. I am me. And that's WHY my husband CHOSE me.

To live in another woman's shadow is to be a shadow of my own self. What purpose would that serve, anyway? To permit me those feelings and interactions that my husband had for and with his late wife? Puh-lease. Had he not endured the loss of a spouse, he would not have the same needs, desires, or hopes for the future that he shares with me. Had he not evolved from his life experiences, then perhaps a clone of his late wife would have suited him best. But he has grown, and is wiser, more patient, and more appreciative of life. Simply put, he is not the same man who lost a spouse several years ago, nor is he the same man who was happily married to the woman who came before me…which means that I am best suited for the man he has become.

Yes, we WOWs are the chosen few. We were not manufactured in our husbands' laboratories, nor injected with a potion that read "Cloning Serum". Our men were smart enough to know that there are no two people on this planet that are exactly the same, so wanting a carbon copy of their late wives was not something our husbands used as a measurement by which they made their choices in new life partners.

Of course, these men desired new wives who would understand that grief and loss could co-exist with newfound love, and that their love for us WOWs would never be diminished by the love they still harbored deep in their souls for their late wives. We do understand, and we do not feel threatened by this respectful admonition nor do we feel ripped off by its implications. We just accept it, nurture it, respect it, and make our own wonderful lives, marriages, and memories with these widowers.

If the late wife indeed has a shadow, it is the mark she made on my husband's heart. As all wives do, she had a hand in helping to make him the man he is today…the man I love. How could I resent that? How could I deny the fact that he loved her when doing so would negate the endless depth of character within him that attracted me in the first place? If I live under this shadow, this impression of her life on his, then I do so willingly and gratefully.

But if "living in the late wife's shadow" means that I must forever acquiesce to her memory, that I must forever accept that my husband will never love me as much as he did her, that the person I am will forever be inferior to his former wife, or that our marriage will forever pale in comparison to what "they" shared, then it would not have been me whom my husband chose...nor would I have chosen him. Those would be impossible requests to make of any unique individual. And I don't know of a single, solitary widower who has ever imposed such demands on a WOW. Therefore, my question to you is, why are YOU?

Yours truly,

The WOW

7

IN SICKNESS AND IN HEALTH

There are several ways in which a widower becomes his status: his late wife was either killed accidentally, by suicide, murdered, or died of "natural causes" or as a result of a terminal illness. But no matter how she did eventually pass on, the husband she leaves behind is faced with overwhelmingly confusing feelings about life, health, death, and dying, no matter how he lost her, and this is perhaps why each person grieves differently and at such a different pace. This leaves many complications and ramifications for a new WOW to face in her marriage.

For instance, one can only imagine how guilt would play a role in a survivor's grief when a wife commits suicide or is murdered. This specific widower's journey beyond bereavement could be especially difficult, in that part of his healing process would be learning to trust anyone ever again, especially when a new possible love interest enters his life.

A widower who lost his wife to a fatal accident of some kind may be left to feel that life is unpredictably out of control, and he may find it hard to find love again since he fears the fickle finger of fate will claim his new love right out from under him as well.

A wife who has died a "natural" death or after a terminal illness leaves behind a man who may be so frightened by death-related issues, or in fear of his own inevitable passing, that he may either become obsessive about his own health and of those he loves. Or, he may become indifferent to the pain and suffering of those around him. He has seen the worst, and may feel that nothing could ever come close, so other people's aches and pains are undeserving of his compassion.

"Sara's" Story

My WOW friend, "Sara", is married to a widower who lost his wife to a long and painful bout with cancer.

> *"With my husband, I can verify his fear of death and his pitiful lack of sympathy when someone is ill. Unless they are dying, his compassion runs cold. If I get the flu, I look to him for some compassion and caring, but he treats me like I am a weakling. I feel like shouting, 'What do I have to do to get some attention around here—die?!'. Of course, I'd never say that, and I feel so guilty about thinking it, but it's true. When the kids and I become ill, I have to accept that he will not take care of us, and it's so frustrating. Don't we deserve a husband's and father's love and support when we are ill?"* Sara laments.

> *"I suppose he's just afraid of losing me, or the kids, to death. But where is this iceberg attitude coming from? You'd think he'd do everything he could to make sure that <u>didn't</u> happen! OK, I admit, I'm not going to die of a cold, but he could be a little more sympathetic. But he just shrugs and tells us that we'll get over it, and then goes about his personal business as if we don't count."*

Jenny's Story

On the other end of the spectrum is Sara's neighbor, a WOW named "Jenny", whose husband's late wife died of "natural causes" at the age of 65 years old.

Jenny relates:

> *"Sara's husband is the complete opposite of mine. When I get sick, my husband is all over me with attention. He smothers me with kindness, and while on one hand it is sweet and comforting, it can also be a real problem. How can I feel better when I am constantly worried about him and that fearful look on his face, as if I will die right before his eyes?"*

> *"He instantly becomes the doctor, telling me what I can and cannot do. He'll even go so far as to doubt me when I say that I am starting to feel better. He'll call the doctor with a million questions, then search every medical encyclopedia until he is satisfied that my symptoms are not life-threatening! I can't even go outside of the house until he is convinced that I no longer show any signs of illness".*

Kelly's Story

"Kelly", a newlywed WOW, recalls how her husband's loss affected his health.

She candidly spoke about it this way:

> *"When we were first dating, my previously widowed husband was a health nut. He ran 10 miles a day every morning, and worked out with weights in the evening. I never assumed that he was this way because of losing a wife to diabetes, and I didn't see the signs of an obsession. I just figured he was a young, health-conscious man who wanted to improve his heart and control his weight."*

> *"What clued me in was when, after we married, he started daily monitoring of his blood sugar. He had never had a problem with diabetes in the past, so I was left to assume that he was afraid of dying the way his late wife did. If the reading were not in a normal range that day, he would restrict his diet—and mine—and increase his exercise regimen, until he would fall into bed, exhausted. Any minor ache or pain was reason to visit the doctor, and he slowly became addicted to pain medication."*

> *"I didn't know how to help him. At my request, our family doctor finally intervened and sent him to a psychotherapist. That was last year. Now, my husband is a new man. He still enjoys his workouts, but he is no longer obsessed with his blood sugar readings or his aches and pains, and he has kicked the pain medication addiction. Through counseling, he was able to admit that he feared death because he saw the ugly side of dying with his late wife, and wanted to take control of his own health. The therapist made him see that he could not fool the Grim Reaper, no matter how healthy he was, but that it was not something to fear."*

Kelly, as a WOW, was privy to the awareness of a link between her husband's obsessive behavior and his late wife's death, and moved into action to help her husband deal with the emotional fallout of this kind of grief.

To Get Beyond the Fear Factor

These stories reflect not so much a widower problem as a marital one, and WOW/widower couples should be sensitive to the other's needs while at the same time, be understanding of the "how's" and "why's" of widower indifference, fear, or guilt—the underlying catalysts of their respective behaviors based on previous loss.

Healing begins from within, and a widower who acts out his grief in regard to a loved one's illness through indifference, obsession, or overbearing attention, needs to recognize the reasons behind his actions before he can effectively deal with them. This is where a WOW can either be an asset or a liability.

WOWs are sometimes "on the outside, looking in" when it comes to her marriage to a widower, in that only *she* can recognize the very behaviors that require change. It helps if you, as a loving WOW, talk to your husband at a time when you are NOT experiencing illness. Gently tell him that you feel his actions are based on his loss, and that you want to help ease his transition through his fears. To do nothing and allow his fears to consume him will only serve to erect larger walls of resentment between you and your husband in your relationship.

While you may possibly have to accept that he may never change, you will have at least have shone a light into the dark chasm of his soul, where fear lies, and forced into the light an awareness of an issue that effects not only him, but you and your family as well.

It's never easy to stand by and helplessly watch as your husband struggles with death-related issues. Nor is it easy to deal with being naively dragged into it with him, or becoming an innocent victim of his problem. Sometimes, we WOWs must intervene and find outside help, as Kelly did by asking her family doctor. The widower may resent your interference at first, but will come to appreciate that your efforts were based on your love for him and your concern for his well-being and that of your marriage.

My Experience

My own husband had a hard time dealing with the fact that we needed to draw up our wills, and that he needed more life insurance coverage. Having a minimal, though apparent, fear of death based on losing not only his late wife but his brother and father as well, he found it difficult to do what was necessary for our future in those regards.

Recognizing this, I took matters into my own hands, arranging for the increase in life insurance and setting the appointments with our family lawyer to draw the wills. Begrudgingly, my husband acquiesced, and after it was all over, mentioned that it really wasn't as bad as he thought it would be.

Fear never is! We all have moments of fear, but most of the time, what we imagine is bigger than what becomes the eventual reality. As WOWs, it is sometimes necessary for us to be the ones to face down the fear of our husbands' hearts, and slay the dragon with confidence in our efforts to make improvements to our relationships while guiding our husbands lovingly out of the confusion.

8

HIS KIDS: BECOMING A WOW STEPMOTHER

A stepparent's role is not that of a biological parent, but of a ***real*** parent nonetheless. WOWs should not be quick to replace the late wife as a mother, but to become to the child the closest thing to a mother he or she has got. The WOW who loves her husband accepts that his children are a part of him, which leads her to want to love them, too. Caring for another person's child(ren) is a calling whose role not everyone can play, but I believe that if the desire, respect, and love exist, the WOW will learn to love the widower's children, and they her.

Being privy to the intimate sorrow and pain these children have endued in the past, the WOW wants only the best things in life for her stepchildren's present and future, and desires an active role in helping them to grow and mature into emotionally healthy, productive adults.

Lay The Groundwork BEFORE The Wedding

Being a WOW stepmother has its own unique challenges because death has touched the widower's kids' lives in a profound way, and often changes the family dynamics even before the WOW enters the picture.

The best way to tackle potential step parenting problems is ***before*** the family is joined in remarriage, with good family communication, or family counseling with an accredited family counselor or minister. Without addressing potential problems up front, the WOW may be unfairly placed in situations she is ill equipped to handle. Again, researching and understanding grief, especially children's grief issues, will prove to be vital in your new role as a stepparent.

In foregoing premarital family counseling, WOWs will be faced with young children who have experienced the death of a parent and may view their surviving parent's remarriage as a betrayal of their beloved mother. They may do their best to make the WOW's transition into the family fold a difficult one. Also, a WOW may feel as if she is playing an emotional tug-of-war between her husband and her stepchildren. She feels placed in the middle, and finds it hard to accept that her role is undefined and often unwelcome.

The Biggest WOW Stepmom Challenge

Most WOWs tell me that if they had to pinpoint one thing they've had to put up with as a stepmother, it would be the extent to which their husbands have overly protected his children. More often than not, a widower feels that he must become for his children their "emotional everything" since the cornerstone of their family unit—their mother—was lost. If the children have not had grief counseling or other counseling of any kind, they are prone to fits and starts when it comes to dealing with their emotional maturity, sense of well-being, and security.

Many times, mostly out of necessity, widowers with minor children have had to assume the role of both father and mother after the late wife passes away. However, this can sometimes create problems when the WOW enters their lives. A widower feels sorry for the children's loss of their mother.

Although kind-hearted and well-meaning, his overprotective nature, and the resulting damage to the children's emotional growth, can sometimes give rise to inappropriate behaviors by his children, including the inability to express themselves properly, a confused sense of "family" and their role in it, or an inability to deal with the opposite sex in appropriate ways.

My WOW friend "Susie" explains her 17year old stepdaughter's behavior this way:

> *"Her way of showing anger is through passive aggression and manipulation. I really feel that, had she been given an appropriate outlet for her anger, grief and sadness, she would be a healthier person, emotionally. He overly pitied her and didn't want her to feel sad, so grief was never discussed in their home before I came along. My husband smothered her with his overprotection, and as a result, she did not have the opportunity to get in touch with her feelings."*

My Best Friend—Dad!

The widower and his daughter sometimes experience a change in their former "father/daughter" relationship because of their mutual loss of the emotional "rock" of their lives. They sometimes turn to each other and assume the role that is missing in the other's life. In other words, the daughter may take on the role of the wife and/or mother, while the widower takes on the role of the mother and/or best friend of his daughter.

Susie goes on to discuss her husband and his daughter:

> *"Since his wife died 6 years ago, my husband has treated his daughter as though she were an adult, so she came to see herself as a peer to her dad to the point where she even took on the role of parent to her younger brother. This was inappropriate of him to do. His daughter lost her mom, and then she sort of lost her Dad, too, since he stopped being a father figure and started being a pal."*

When the WOW enters their lives, the children's repressed and unresolved emotions are often outwardly exhibited in the form of jealousy, competitiveness, or feeling that they must protect their father from any further pain as well. They view the WOW as a threat, more than a helpmate, to her husband. And they fear that the WOW will monopolize their father's love and time, leaving them nothing at a time when they are most confused about their father's moving on with his life and remarrying.

Another WOW friend, "Janine", still struggles with the fallout of her 16 year old stepdaughter's grief in relation to the child's father:

> *"To this day, my stepdaughter has a tendency to want too much "alone time" with her father. She doesn't want anyone else around when she is talking to him,*

just like the old days when he devoted all his attention to her. There is definitely a possessive element to her relationship with him. Sure, I want them to have a close relationship, and I am not jealous of the time they spend together. It's just that I look at them from an "outsider's" point of view. From my vantage point, I feel that my stepdaughter's hold on her father is not healthy, even though it is understandable because of their mutual grief. And yet, how does a WOW express her concerns regarding this issue without sounding possessive herself?!"

What a horrible term, "emotional incest"—but that's precisely what it is. The daughter begins to see herself as a partner in the household, while the father may unintentionally encourage it because of his own emotional needs, his fear, and his guilt-parenting.

Daddy's Little Girl

Susie agrees that emotional incest is a problem in her life as well, and adds another aspect—that of worrying about her stepdaughter's relationship with other men in the girl's life:

"I also fear that my stepdaughter will have trouble in her future relationships with men, and I believe that this is also a direct result of her mother's death and her dad's subsequent handling of all things emotional and behavioral. She has grown so accustomed to living in a home with 2 males who pretty much put up with anything she did, that she is already having trouble getting along with the opposite sex. In the past year, she has had three relationships that were more than platonic. Every one of them ended almost before they had begun, and she has blamed the males every time. They are either not attentive enough, not loving enough…always somehow lacking. I feel that she has unrealistic expectations with regard to men; like she expects men to treat her in the same way her dad has for years. And I also think there is some confusion with her feeling that she is being disloyal to her dad by going out with guys. I say this because my husband has treated his daughter more like a pseudo-partner than a daughter before I came along."

The Teenaged WOW Stepson

Sons of widowers are often not as conflicted as a whole, but still have issues unique to their gender depending on their age at the time of loss. Everyone has watched an old western movie and cringed when the bereaved widow turns to her small son and says, "*Well, looks like you're the man of the house now!*" imposing an unnecessary and life-altering burden on the child. But even without it being said out loud, a widow or widower's son, especially a teen or preteen, will sometimes assume that role without being asked.

In doing so, the child not only becomes an instant adult, but also is forced to forge ahead without dealing with his own grief appropriately. He regards his grieving father compassionately but unrealistically as an emotional cripple, and feels it necessary to be the stronger male in the house in order to hold it all together. Sometimes a widower subconsciously allows this, as he feels his burden ease somewhat because of his son's take-charge attitude. This, in turn, breeds a son who now feels such a strong commitment and responsibility to his father, brothers and/or sisters that he sacrifices his youth for them. When the WOW enters this family dynamic, she often finds it difficult to deal with a new stepson who is still a child, but who suffers from major control issues.

My WOW friend "Gail" speaks of her relationship with her stepson this way:

> "*My stepson was 15 years old when his father and I met. Looking at him, I would have correctly guessed his age. But speaking to him, and watching him interact with his family and with other adults, I would have thought he was 30 years old! He has no buddies to speak of, since he finds them boring and immature. Small wonder! This boy has been forced to be a man since he was 12 years old, since his mother's death! He feels out of place in the world. Now that he has graduated from high school, he has the grades to go to any Ivy League university of his choosing, but he doesn't want to go! He feels that his family needs him, and that our home is where he belongs.*"

> "*When his father and I had our first date, my now-stepson actually told us what time to be home! I looked to his father to correct him, but my now-husband just said, 'OK, son. Will do'. Then, after we had been going out for a few weeks, I noticed that my husband's son actually took care of all the household expenses and paid the bills, and often cooked dinner. He even screened his sister's dates! This is not appropriate behavior for a child, and his father has just gone along with him. My husband has felt that allowing my stepson to assume an adult role in the house has taught him responsibility, so he has encouraged it. But I can see the damage this has done to the boy.*"

Mommy's Little Boy Lost

Little boys under the age of 12 have their own issues as well. Unfortunately, they are raised in a society that scorns a man's tears, so while a little boy may grieve the loss of his "mommy", he does so privately, so as not to incur the snickers and taunts of his peers should he outwardly show his emotions. This burying of grief emotions is unhealthy, especially if the widower who cannot handle the sadness of his children rules that any discussion of grief or of their dead mother will not be tolerated in the home.

When a WOW marries a widower with such a son, she represents to the boy a sure sign that his mother is indeed gone forever, thus ending his dream of being reunited with her. Also, he may feel confused, thinking that perhaps Daddy didn't really love Mommy if he was so eager to replace her. At that point, his grief, no matter how long his mother has been gone, may increase. The WOW may then be dealing with a boy who is resentful of her presence, and act out in naughty behavior. He may truly want to love and accept the WOW, but thinks doing so betrays his beloved mother and may also put him at risk of losing another "mother" as well.

Sometimes, a WOW's stepson of this age presents an opposite behavior and becomes possessive of the WOW. He has yearned for a mother substitute and all the wonderful "warm and fuzzy" feelings he remembers from his mother. In his desperation to be loved, especially by a new mother, he manipulates her time and smothers her with his affections and attention. He feels a need to possess her, thinking that his love can shield her from death. And often, he is confused about his father's love of her, viewing it as a competition for her.

Dad's Emotional Roller Coaster

Another WOW issue regarding step parenting is often about the widower himself. While he may love his new wife dearly, he carries with him an enormous amount of guilt, more often than not imposed upon him by the children themselves or perhaps by the children's mother's family: he struggles with everyone's lack of approval of his new wife and with trying to please everyone in a household where no one is in agreement. When it comes to the WOW, his heart breaks when his precious little ones cry, *"But she's NOT my mother!"* or *"Why do we need HER? We were just fine before SHE came along!"* or *"You can't make me love her!"*

He deals with his own grief issues while the guilt feeds his idea of selfishness for deciding to love again since it is apparently hurting his children so. He also wonders if he has indeed betrayed his late wife by loving again. And the guilt goes on.

Perhaps he also misses the loving family unit that once was since his new household may be in such a negative upheaval. He may find it hard to relinquish the overprotective role he is so used to playing in order to "side" with his children, relegating the WOW to a lower rung on the family ladder than that of the family dog. He may even believe that his loyalties lie with his "real family"—his children—and that any perceived interference as the WOW takes her place in the family as a disciplinarian or loving mother figure may anger him or confuse him even further.

Communication=Hope!

While not every step parenting situation in WOWdom will be as negative as these WOW's, it is best to be prepared for the worst case scenario, do your research, find a qualified family therapist, and communicate with frank, open discussions with the adults and children in the family as soon as and often as possible.

It helps immensely if the WOW and her husband create a united front for the children, but the road to such skillful parenting must be precipitated by intense communication between the WOW and her husband, especially *before* the wedding. It is then that the WOW's role as a stepmother will begin to be defined, and then implemented, in unison with her husband.

9

THE BABY STEP

As I have mentioned before, my husband's late wife did not bear him children. But as long as he can remember, my husband has always dreamed of being a father. He had a wonderful childhood, and a close relationship with his own father. His parents' marriage was a good one, and he and his siblings got along famously. All of this factored into his decision to pursue fatherhood, even after his late wife learned of her terminal illness, by attempting, but ultimately failing, to adopt.

Does The Dream Have To Die, Too?

One of the most difficult things about losing a spouse is that not only does one lose love and companionship when the spouse dies, but also the dreams that were shared with that beloved spouse. Often, parenthood is one of those dreams that never become a reality for the widower, and it is a fate that becomes a bitter pill if the widower has been obsessed with attaining his dream of parenthood. Quite often, a man looks upon fathering a child as his chance to leave a legacy of himself behind.

When a spouse dies without having been able to grant this wish, the widower's grief is twofold: he grieves for the woman who he has lost, and for the dreams that were buried with her. The hopelessness of his situation takes on a new shape, and it sometimes feeds an obsession to acquire that which he has spent a lifetime pursuing but not achieving.

When a WOW enters his life, a widower may still desire children, and looks upon his new wife with new hope. In being a step parent, my husband's wish of becoming a father had been somewhat fulfilled, and he has tried very hard to be the best dad he can be to children who are not his by genetics. Still, the legacy belongs to the children's birth father, so my husband's dream of parenthood, though somewhat quenched, had not been fully sated.

Decisions, Decisions!

As his wife, I naturally wanted to help make all my husband's dreams come true. But at age 40, I wasn't sure if having a baby with him was something I wanted to go through again. We would be middle-aged parents! There were statistics of age-related genetic abnormalities to consider, as well as thinking of how our ages would factor into our future plans. Our scariest (and silliest!) thought was of dying before our child graduated from high school! And how would society feel about us old-timers spinning the genetic wheel once more? Would our child be faced with people absent-mindedly assuming that we were his or her *grandparents* instead of "Mom" and "Dad"?

There were also financial considerations, too. My husband and I were at a point in our pre-marriage lives where we could finally see through the cloud of debt and put some money aside for college expenses, retirement, the future in general, and our dreams of buying a boat and a cottage in the northern country of Canada. Would having a baby be like trading one dream for another? A new baby would most definitely be a source of financial stress for many years to come.

Also to be considered was the possibility that perhaps we would not be able to conceive, leading to tremendous self-imposed guilt feelings on my part for failing to make my husband a daddy. How far, financially and mentally, were we willing to go to try and conceive? We knew that, technologically speaking, attempting to conceive in artificial ways would be straining and draining, and still may lead to failure and disappointment month after grueling month. If conception was not possible, my husband's fatherhood dreams would this time not only be postponed but also trashed, perhaps leading to a depression that would cause him and our marriage great pain and problems.

On The Positive Side

As a WOW, you and your husband must decide for yourselves, based on your own unique situation, if having a baby together is right for you. For us, this was a decision that was not to be made in haste or taken lightly. But neither was it one that only bore negative factors.

On the plus side, having a child with my husband was something that I knew would serve as a bond between us, strengthening our marital union. And while the thought of being middle-aged parents had its drawbacks, there would be blessings. We were wiser, more mature, and more "life experienced" than we had been in our youths. We would be sharing the job of parenting a part of each other's souls—forever nurturing together a child born out of love and deep desire for his/her being. This baby would be the most wanted child on earth.

Having been a mother prior to marrying my husband, I knew all too well what to expect—the good, the bad, and the ugly. I was experienced, which could only benefit my husband as a father, too. And, I wasn't too bitter about my divorce from my children's father to remember what a beautiful experience having a baby with someone you love can be. I wanted to share that with my husband. And I romantically felt that we had enough love between us and in our family to overcome any obstacles that might stand in our way.

WOW Considerations

As a WOW, I also selfishly considered that by having my husband's child, I would be giving him a gift that his late wife could/did not, making me feel very erroneously superior to her in that respect. It was a thought that made me grin with delight, knowing that being the mother of his only child would be something unique only to he and I—something that would put ME up on the pedestal he usually only reserved in her name. Parenting our own child together would most definitely put "her" on the back burner of his heart, and move me into my rightful position!

But I digressed. The temporary insanity of my selfishness eventually gave way to compassion and intelligence, and I remembered that our decision would have to be made with the utmost respect for each other, our future, and our marriage, without selfish thoughts and insecurities superseding either. We would have to consider all the medical information, the "what if?"s of being middle aged parents, and the money pit created by new babies—and we would have to think about each factor emotionally, intellectually, and spiritually, before making the commitment. But we would have to decide quickly since we weren't getting any younger!

Andersen, Party Of…FIVE?!

We would have to consider the feelings of my other children as well, since having a new baby in the house would profoundly affect their lives. And they had already been through so much—being the children of divorce, moving to a foreign country, and acquiring a new stepfather and a new kind of family situation. Having had Mom all to themselves for years only to be forced to relinquish that time to a new baby, would the older children come to resent me, their stepfather, or our seemingly selfish decision? Would they be concerned about their place in this new family, feeling like outsiders under their own roof? Would the age difference of 7 and 10 years make it hard for them to bond with a sibling they may not have much time for in their busy lives, and not many years to bond with before going off to college?

While preparing my children for the possibility of another sibling and yet another change in their lives, I was reminded that my children had always been unnaturally unselfish as far as kids go. We had always had great communication between us, and had always tried out our best to consider each other's feelings when a change was about to take place in our lives. The kids were very positive about the idea, and spent days upon end excitedly sharing with each other and with us all the great "big brother/big sister" stuff they would do with and for a new baby.

God's Perfect Plan

It's always amused me that no matter how carefully people plan something, God reveals his will and makes the decision for them! This was true in our case, as the rabbit died before we made an intelligent "yes" or "no" decision about becoming parents! I remember driving home from the doctor's office, afraid that my husband would be angry, or disappointed, or so worried about me and our future that he would have a mental breakdown! But the smile on my husband's face and the tears of utter joy in his eyes when I told him the blessed news calmed all my fears. As usual, God had made the right decision. Now, we just had to trust that He would see us through.

And, He did! Barring the usual pregnancy-related aches and pains, and the fact that my age did make it a bit harder to carry this baby even though I was as healthy as a horse, our daughter blessed the world and our hearts at the end of 1999 with her arrival, surrounded by her whole family—me, her daddy, her brother, and her sister.

The doctor who delivered our baby was the same doctor who had cared for my husband's late wife during her struggle with cancer. Our joy was almost matched by hers as she watched the big, strong hands of my emotionally overcome husband cradling his dream come true, knowing personally what he had endured to acquire it. I was instantly enveloped with a feeling of reassurance that we had done a good thing...the *right* thing...in giving birth to her. Whatever it would take, my husband and I were ready to devote everything to this gift of a second chance at a dream.

And when she took her first breath, I knew that my baby was also surrounded by those who came before her—those whose sacrifices and love aided in her creation: my husband's deceased father and his late wife. As I held this awesome wonder in my arms minutes after she screamed her mighty lungs into life, bathing in the intimacy only understood by brand new parents, I lovingly whispered to my husband that his new daughter had been kissed by his lost loved ones on her way out of Heaven and into our lives; that today on this, his daughter's birth day, his deceased loved ones danced and sang with the angels in celebration of new life: our baby's...and our own. It was, truly, a "family" moment.

10

DEALING WITH FAMILY

I don't know any genuinely evil people personally. That doesn't mean I don't think they exist, but most people I have come into contact with are good-hearted and well meaning by nature. I think most people who cannot be truly sympathetic, perhaps because they simply cannot relate, are at least compassionate and empathetic, and try their hardest not to be hurtful.

Nevertheless, many WOWs experience ignorant comments from otherwise kind-hearted people throughout the course of their marriages. Alas, some really ARE mean-spirited and intentional, too. And some disparaging comments come from family members as well.

Terry's Story

One good example of how seemingly innocent comments can sting a WOW's heart is my WOW friend, "Terry". Terry's husband lost his wife about seven years prior to meeting her. By that time, you'd think that his family and friends would welcome a new love into his life with open arms. But alas, Terry has endured some unbelievable comments from people, and she related to me recently this story about her wedding last year and the dark cloud that had hung over her otherwise perfect day:

> *"My brother-in-law, among others, felt the need to interrupt our wedding dance just to tell me how happy my husband was—in his FIRST marriage! He droned on and on about how wonderful his brother's late wife was, and what a great couple they made. Here it was, OUR special day, and yet because of these ref-*

erences to the past, it sometimes felt more like a memorial than a day of celebration".

"Before we were married, people seemed to view me suspiciously, as if I was trying to take advantage of a poor, defenseless widower in his grief. And because of their preconceived notions, I believe that their snide remarks were intentional. Why can't they just accept that he has moved on, and treat me with some respect for loving the person he is and wanting to share my life with him?"

Why, indeed!

The "Former" In-Laws

We'd all love to be accepted into our significant other's family circle. But the sad truth is that, for the WOW, coming to terms with these people from our husbands' past life is sometimes yet another hurdle to overcome, if at all.

It is often difficult for the late wife's family to welcome the WOW with open arms, simply because they may perceive her as a threat to their loved one's memory, making the WOW the enemy who dares to negate the late wife's existence and importance just because the widower loves her and has chosen her as his new soul mate in life. This leads to a very awkward "love/hate" relationship with these particular "family members".

The late wife's parents may have felt for their son-in-law, the WOW's husband, as their own son. So while they may truly want him to be happy even without their daughter in his daily life, they know that the trade-off means accepting his having moved forward with his life and loving someone else, and may come to view the WOW as "the other woman" who forced their daughter's husband to betray his late wife. The family may fear that the WOW will knock the late wife off of her much-deserved (in their minds) pedestal, relegating her to a lower hierarchy in the family chain, or negating her existence altogether.

If there were children to "their" marriage, the WOW will be marrying part of the late wife's family—like it or not—and she will have to deal with another set of "in-laws". They have a right to visit with their grandchildren/nieces/nephews even though the widower is legally no longer part of their family. In the family's eyes, because of the connection to these children through the widower as the father, he is still considered "family" to them, and like most families, they only want what's best for him because they love him. Problem is, perhaps the only "best thing" that would satisfy them is a return of the late wife!

Strange as it sounds, they may have a hard time accepting the WOW because doing so would mean accepting that their deceased daughter was not the "saint" who could forever be immortalized by her husband's celibacy and/or faithfulness had he remained single and myopically focused on only her.

The late wife's parents may appear to be pessimistic about the seriousness and depth of the love the WOW has for her husband, and he for her. They may not be able to accept that any other woman besides their beloved daughter could make the widower as happy, fulfilled, or loved. In their eyes, the WOW may represent a "substitute" for the daughter/sister they loved, and a poor one at that. They may never accept that the WOW is good enough for their son-in-law, or as good as their late daughter since, to them, she was the best and only person who could fill that role.

The Widower's Family

The widower's immediate family may be thrilled that he has found someone to love with all his heart, and that he is beyond bereavement now, so they can stop worrying so much about him. They may be so appreciative of what the WOW-to-be has done to make him so happy that they throw their arms around her and welcome her into the family fold without incident.

My husband's family was wonderful to me from the very beginning, and I think they are role models of how a loving family should treat a newcomer. They respect my boundaries, and I respect their grief. They have accepted me for the person I am, and have never perceived me as the late wife's replacement.

If this is not what you have experienced as a WOW with your husband's family, however, remember that the widower's immediate family—parents, sisters and brothers, etc.—have also experienced a loss. They may have dearly loved the late wife, and considered her an addition to their own family, so her death was also a tragedy for them as well. And in a way, they also "lost" their son, brother, uncle, etc., albeit temporarily. They were not only affected by her loss, but also by HIS loss, his grief, and his sadness.

Loving him like they do, they may have done everything in their power to ease his pain and suffering. They may have taken him under their protective family wings and tried to nurture him through his anguish. They may have tried to make sure he was never alone for too long. They probably encouraged him to cry and to laugh. They may have tried to help him find some "normalcy" in his upturned world just by staying close by. They may also have enjoyed feeling so needed by him.

They may have worried about him—that he might never "shake" his grief and move forward with his life. They probably hoped he would find happiness again. But did they ever dream that he would remarry to do just that? Probably not…and most definitely not as soon as they believed was right!

Just like the widower's former in-laws, perhaps his immediate family is just as suspicious of the next woman to come into his life. Perhaps they think his remarrying is "too soon" (whatever THAT is!) after his late wife's death. They may want to protect him from any further pain, and may "size up the competition" (the WOW-to-be) before she even gets through their front doors! They may even go so far as to pull the WOW-to-be aside and lecture her about not messing around with the heart of this man, their poor family member, who had just lost his beloved wife.

They may even be jealous of the WOW-to-be, the new love of the widower's heart, since she supplies his needs now, and perhaps this makes the family resentful about relinquishing a role they have since cherished. They may not give the WOW-to-be the chance she deserves because they still remember the late wife so clearly, and may feel that the WOW-to-be will never measure up or contribute to the family's well-being and unity simply because she is so different.

Remember To Empathize

We, as WOWs, must remember that these people, the families of the late wife and of her widower, have undergone a terrible tragedy in their lives, and that loss has left a huge impression, perhaps leaving them feeling vulnerable and out of control of their emotions, no matter how much time has passed. We must also remember that for these people, the late wife was not only deeply loved but often seen as "perfect" in their eyes, as survivors tend to forget the deceased's flaws and faults after she passes.

While this must never excuse any intentionally nasty behavior by them, being empathetic to their grief must be a consideration when we are faced with negativity on their part. We must be respectful of the late wife's memory while in their presence, as we would be towards anyone who has experienced the loss of a loved one. We must allow time to heal their wounds, as we must also allow time for them to accept what they cannot change. We must continue to be true to ourselves as individuals, and pray that the day will come when we are accepted as such.

I cannot stress enough how vitally important it is for you, as a WOW or WOW-to-be, to do your homework and try to comprehend the nature of grief. You will be more capable of understanding that your husband's past and present family members are dealing with their own set of grief issues, just as you are. The knowledge of that fact makes compassion come easily.

You may also be one of the lucky WOWs whose late wife's relatives welcome you into the "family" and treat you with every kindness. I believe these people are angels on earth, for they have felt death's sting and have learned to cope with its grief enough to realize that love never dies, it just grows more beautifully as it is shared, and becomes a legacy of their deceased loved one's life. They are the parents/siblings who understand that their daughter/sister would have wanted her husband to love again and be happy. Consider yourself blessed to have such strong, wonderful people to call "family".

I'd like to think that late wives would want it this way. If true love means wanting the best for the other person in your relationship, then she would want her husband to be happy, and her family to accommodate him and respect his choices. And truly, if the family knew their daughter well, then they would be accepting of the WOW, knowing that she is a representation of a continuation of love that is not divided when shared.

Draw Them Close?...

Patience does not come easily—it comes with practice. But does a WOW really have to accept the late wife's relatives into her life and into her new union with her husband? Are these people really necessary in her new life and marriage? I think the answer to that depends a lot on the individual widowers and WOWs. Each have special circumstances in their unique situations, so because of this, there is no "one-size-fits-all" solution.

In many cases, a widower husband did not have children with his late wife, so a WOW would not have stepchildren to raise who would inevitably have tied me to their mother's family, making detaching from them almost impossible. However, even though the extended family felt close to him at one time, a widower's late wife's family may find it difficult to accept the WOW in the way that he had hoped, so he may cut all ties with them, slowly and methodically. Although civil and respectful of each other, they are no longer the family of old, which is, of course, the root of the problem.

Of course, many WOWs will feel enormous guilt over this, and beg their husbands to reconsider, allowing that she wouldn't mind if he alone continued communications with them, even if they would never come to accept her. But a widower in this position feels that since he and his new wife are "one flesh" by way of marriage, then she is "part and parcel" of the whole package. For her husband, it becomes an "all-or-nothing" proposition: either they learn to accept her, or they lose us both.

I am glad that many remarried widowers choose to take the reins in this situation, because I believe it is imperative for the widower to play an integral part in joining (or disjoining) the late wife's family to (or from) his new wife. He must be strong enough of spirit and character to be able to make a stand for his new wife. By doing so, he is then capable of either being the bridge across troubled waters in acting as the cornerstone from which their relationship will build, or he will act as the negotiator in bringing about a compromise.

It *is* possible. I have seen it work, and I believe that the bereaved family who offers and olive branch to a WOW will find a new kind of family member to embrace—a WOW who wants to love them as part of her extended family because she respects and understands the late wife's important existence if, in return, she is guaranteed their acknowledgment of her own individuality and importance as well.

...Or Cut Them Loose?

I don't believe that it is necessary to cut ties with the late wife's family altogether. I believe in compromises (*OK, you can haul out the family albums in my presence if you really want to*), boundaries (*No, I will not allow you, at family gatherings, to start any sentence about the late wife in front of me with, "Remember when...?"*), and comfort levels that must be respected by all parties, and if all the people involved can hammer out an acceptable agreement, then why shouldn't they all be friends?

But what if a compromise cannot be met? What if there really ARE intentionally mean-spirited people who must be dealt with—those who cannot seem to overcome their own grief issues or let go of the past enough to accept the WOW as the person she is? Should we WOWs continue to suffer their slings and arrows in silence out of respect for the deceased or our own husbands?

Absolutely not! I believe in detaching from toxic people whenever possible for good mental health, no matter who they are.

Melanie's Story

For example, my WOW friend "Melanie"'s husband finally became a daddy when they had their own baby together two years ago. At that time, they announced their daughter's arrival in the local newspaper. Perhaps it was just coincidence, but I believe that reading it prompted Melanie's husband's late wife's sister (who had always maintained a civil and friendly relationship with Melanie's husband) to call him from a two year absence and demand the return of a few of her sister's (the late wife's) costume jewelry and other trivial effects.

When her husband refused, reminding his former sister-in-law that his late wife's will had already been deposed to everyone's satisfaction three years prior, she threatened legal action, screamed obscenities into the phone, and called back many times over several days to do the same. And while even Melanie intervened and tried to smooth out the situation, it was no use. She and her husband both needed to detach from this woman for their own peace of mind, so they gave her what she wanted, and have never heard from her since.

I believe that perhaps the birth announcement was just too much for the late wife's sister to bear. Maybe it was a kick in her ribs by the old Grief Monster. Maybe she was sad to think that her sister would never be a mother, or herself an aunt, and her jealousy over the widower's baby's birth was tormenting to her. I sympathize with that. But as much as I can empathize and try to analyze her, the bottom line is clear—no one should be forced to "take it on the chin" if they have done nothing wrong. If toxic people cannot find a way to rid themselves of their own inner demons and continually wreak havoc in the lives of the widower and the WOW, then total or temporary detachment becomes not only understandable, but also necessary.

Taking Matters Into Your Own Hands

My friend Terry's husband's former in-laws felt threatened by her from the start, and they were angry with her husband for even considering remarrying. Terry eventually took matters into her own hands one day before her wedding when she approached the late wife's mother, took her hand, looked her straight in the eye and sympathetically said,

> "I am not here to erase your daughter's memory, or take her place in any way. She was a unique and special person...and so am I! I just want you to know that your daughter will always be welcome in our home and in my husband's heart. You must have loved her very much to be missing her so much. I really wish I could have known her".

And with that, the two women hugged and cried. Although they are not what you would call "close", the late wife's mother speaks of Terry kindly, respects her boundaries, and even came to her wedding to wish Terry and her former son-in-law well.

There is nothing like grace, forgiveness, and love to break down the barriers that stand between good people who cannot seem to connect. We are all prone to being unapproachable to some degree, and sometimes feel loathe allowing the bull into our china shop of vulnerability. So we build walls around our hearts to protect ourselves. But those walls really do not serve us well. They only keep us divided and separated from what may be very special relationships with very special people.

Only *you* know your own unique situation well enough to decide how to proceed with either mending the fences or building a permanent wall. The choice is yours to make, but to do nothing may either breed indifference or allow wounds to fester. Doing something, either by direct or indirect channels, at least shows you care enough about all parties, including yourself, to make a positive change happen.

Grief is a complex human emotion, and while we may think that these reactions to a new WOW are thoughtless and unkind, they are nonetheless normal for people experiencing bereavement who may still be walking the path of their own personal grief journey. Our responsibility as WOWs is to understand this, and then deal with the families from our husband's past and present as humanely and as sensitively as possible.

11

COMPARING THE SECOND WIFE AND THE WOW

Apparently, some people believe that a WOW and her issues is/are the same for a second wife to a divorced man, and since there are hundreds of books dealing with remarriage in general, why can't WOWs just read those?

In trying to understand the role of the WOW, society must first come to terms with the uniqueness of her situation. It is indeed rather different from being the second wife of a divorced man.

Similarities

When comparing the second wife of a divorced man to a WOW, let me start out by saying that neither of us has it any easier. We just have different issues that we bring to the marital table.

The similarities are basically the same: we get to live with all the emotional baggage of the past; we are forced to make compromises about and live with some of the first wives' possessions; we get to help raise her children, if there are any; we are both faced with "former" relatives; we have to learn to adjust to these men who say they love us, while at the same time acknowledging that we were not their first choice in the marriage department; we both struggle with insecurities about and comparisons to the first wives.

The differences lie somewhere between the emotions of the new husbands and the context of their prior relationships.

Differences

Wives of widowers live with the idea that their husbands did not choose to live without their late wives. In contrast, the divorced man either chose to end his marriage, or his ex wife chose to not be with him, or it was mutual.

Either way, a second wife to a divorced man receives comfort in knowing that her husband doesn't want his first wife anymore and that she, the second wife, is his chosen one and the love of his life. A widower would, in most cases, still want to be with his late wife had she not died. There was no choice to end the marriage. So WOWs end up feeling like second best or not really what their husbands would have chosen the first time around.

With divorce, there are usually bad memories in the end of the relationship. A second wife can verify this by the degree of animosity between her husband and his ex-wife. With death, there are usually no bad memories in regard to the relationship, and even if there were, it is still considered a no-no to speak ill of the dead, so a deceased spouse is often unrealistically canonized in death. Because of this, WOWs often have to deal with husbands that can't always recall that their first wives were not saints, since the widower's late wife passed away while the widower and she were still very much in love.

WOWs battle things unseen, having to wonder about a special person from their husbands' past that they often never knew. Divorced men are more realistic—more often than not, they know for sure that their ex wives were not holier-than-thou because the first wife is still very much alive for the second wife to view, "warts and all". A WOW only has the glowing reviews from her husband and others to go by. Following a "saint" is difficult and daunting for a human being complete with faults and failures, but many WOWs endure this kind of comparison in their marriages.

Facing a Ghost Vs. Facing The Real Thing

The second wife of a divorced man has the opportunity to "see" her predecessor, and come to fully understand how life would have been for her husband had he stayed with his ex-wife, making the ex-wife less of a threat to her marriage.

The WOW understands fully that she would not be married to her husband had his first wife remained alive, and has to assume many things that are not revealed to her about the late wife's personality or how successful a wife she really was, or how successful the marriage of her and the widower. Because of this lack of information, a WOW, when comparing her role as "wife" to that of her predecessor, often feels she comes up short, thereby feeling just as threatened by the late wife as some second wives view their husbands' ex-wives.

Second wives of divorced men get to live with all of the pain and drama that their husbands' ex-wives often intentionally inflict on them. If there are stepchildren involved, the second wives get to share their lives with the ex-wives every day because of their shared interest in the children. And sometimes, they get to deal with the guilt and the "I'm a bad guy" frustrations that their men carry around if they were the ones who initiated divorce with their ex-wives. This guilt makes them putty in the hands of their children and their ex-wives, leaving the second wife to live with their manipulation.

WOWs deal with a different kind of guilt with their husbands—"survivor's guilt". The widower often feels that his choice to remarry is a betrayal of his late wife and her memory. Survivor's guilt also often includes powerless feelings that the widower was not able to "save" his wife from death because he could not control what happened, and that perhaps it should have been he himself instead of her to suffer so needlessly. This guilt may be all consuming or occasional, but it often hampers the widower's giving of himself completely to his second wife.

Substitute Mom?

A WOW stepmother feels that society will never come to accept her role as "mother". The role of the deceased mother is viewed as sacred, and invading that space is usually not looked upon kindly. WOWs often get much more criticism in the beginning of their marriages than they do support.

Often, people are constantly worried about the children and how THEY are coping with their mother's death and their father's remarriage, ignoring the WOW's feelings as she struggles with the biggest challenge of her life. This is often true for second wives of divorced men as well, since the biological mother of a divorced man's children is usually still actively involved in her child(ren)'s life to some degree. However, a late wife is no longer present in the lives of her child(ren).

Both the second wife and the WOW can sometimes feel like they are in "damned if I do, damned if I don't" situations, in that people expect them to raise the children in the same manner as the first wife. But this is unrealistic because it is impossible. All parties of both scenarios are distinct in their parenting styles because they all have unique personalities and past experiences to go by when it comes to parenting.

These are but a few of the similarities and differences faced by second wives of divorced men and WOWs. But by comparing the two unique roles, it is my hope that society will learn to understand just why a book about WOWs and their issues is necessary—because for WOWs, there is a need for uplifting and enlightening information, but mostly a need for validation, acceptance, and respect for their role in society, since it IS so very different than that of any other category of "second wife".

12

DEALING WITH SOCIETY'S VIEW OF THE WOW

I once had the remarkable opportunity to participate in a women's opinion poll regarding remarriage. The questions posed were, "If your husband died, would you remarry?" and, "Do you think your husband would remarry if you died?" The results were rather typical of a two-part poll: nearly half of the respondents felt that they would remarry while the other half did not, and an equal number felt the same held true for their husbands.

However, what shocked me as a WOW were the conclusions that could be made from the additional comments some of the ladies wrote, who felt that neither they nor their husbands…would ever remarry.

"No, I would not remarry."

"No one could take his place."

"I love him so much, I don't know that I would ever feel that way about anyone else again—if I didn't love him the way I did my husband."

"I would remarry if my next husband loved me the way I am loved now. He (my present husband) would be a very tough act to follow."

"Until I met my husband, I never believed in soul mates, but he is mine and no one else could ever be."

"My husband says that he couldn't remarry, even if he met someone whose company he enjoyed. The love would pale in comparison to what he felt for me and he couldn't cheat himself and someone else out of true love and total commitment."

"It would be difficult to try and build a relationship with someone while all along knowing that you used to have something better."

"I can't imagine finding another person just like my husband in every way, so I do not think I would remarry."

Drawing My Conclusions

Sound familiar? Even I have to admit that I have spoken similar words in the past. It is hard to imagine what one would do when faced with the loss of a spouse; so all the above comments are simply mere conjecture, probably based on a deep love that is blind to any possibility of remarriage.

However, these comments do somewhat represent the opinions of our society as a whole overall, and have led me to conclude that from society's point of view, we WOWs are apparently mere substitutions or replacements for the "real" loves" (the late wives) of our husband's lives. We apparently settle for second place in our husbands' hearts, with our limp and lifeless marriages suffering a missing component compared to what our previously widowed husbands had before with their late wives. Those who have never walked in WOW shoes also apparently assume that the WOW must be a carbon copy of the late wife, since an "outsider" looks upon the first wife as that great love of her husband's heart, and no one loving him after her will ever come as close.

One can also conclude from this poll society's assumptions about a previously widowed husband: that he must have remarried for companionship alone, in order to combat loneliness. Also, he will forever canonize his late wife into saint-hood, thus dismissing any real intimate or loving feelings to be shared with his second wife as nothing more than the passage of time, since his one and only soul mate is gone and can never be replaced. To the outside world, we WOWs stand in the late wife's stead, garnering even more sympathy for the poor widower who will never be happy again, no matter whom he remarries.

Out Of Sight, But NOT Out Of Mind?

WOWs are seemingly perceived by some as a threat to the memory of the late wives and the love they shared with our husbands, as reflected in the following pollster's comments regarding their husband's likelihood of remarriage:

> *"When I think about this actually happening, I feel territorial for sure. He is mine and I want him to love only me forever and ever and we will always be together and never die."*

> *"I just can't picture him with anyone else but me."*

> *"Personally, right now I'd feel jealous of him being with someone else. I'd want him to miss me and mourn for me forever and never replace me."*

> *"Some part of me really would like to think that he could never love anyone again like he does me, and knowing that, I would hope he would pine away for me and mourn my loss forever."*

Not very comforting to a WOW, to say the least! These reflections only seem to add a new dimension of guilt to the already daunting list of WOW issues, as they reflect a certain resentment toward the poll taker's husbands should these men go on to marry again.

It can also be assumed from the previous quotes that a WOW is a living representation of her husband's lack of credibility regarding the depth of his first marriage, in that it must not have been that great if he was so "eager" to replace her. If this is the case, then society does not give much credit to the resiliency of a widower—the fact that he takes with him into the next marriage the life lessons he has learned, gleaned from, and grown from because of being a survivor, while at the same time NEVER forgetting or negating the love he had for his first wife by remarrying after her death.

Walking In WOW Shoes

But, upon further introspection, one thought remained in the forefront of my mind: that all of these responses were from women who had never dealt with grief or grief-related issues, nor had they experienced the loss of a spouse, and therefore, could not and cannot fathom the extent of the growth and healing that takes place after the death of a husband or a wife.

Not surprisingly, the WOWs who posted responses to the poll had a more self-sacrificial and selfless aspect to both their (and their husbands') death and remarriage possibilities/probabilities. They KNEW, based on their own experiences of being married to widowers, that life indeed MUST go on after loss, and that a surviving spouse CAN appreciate another love again, even more beautifully than before. The WOW respondents wanted their husbands to again move forward after they themselves died, and find yet another wonderfully special WOW to love.

The WOWs who responded to the poll felt that they, too, were capable of moving on and remarrying, knowing that their husbands would never be forgotten or "replaced" should they die, and also acknowledging that their husbands could appreciate and love another wife for her uniqueness and individuality, just as he had accepted each of them, respectively, in their own second marriages.

To build on this, I would like to think that society could come to appreciate the role of the WOW by learning to understand that a man's life choices are based not only upon his mere survival, but also upon fulfilling a kind of happiness quotient that includes a happy, committed, loving relationship.

Coming "Full Circle"

Clearly, everyone wants his or her spouse to think of their loving union as the best, the "only", and the one to outshine the rest—the kind of love that will last into eternity, paling in comparison to anything or anyone who offers a replication. But this is simply not the reality of today's world.

Just as society must come full circle with issues such as intolerance and racism because of the harm their ignorance breeds, society must also be educated about, and learn to accept, the widower's choice in a second wife, his reasons for choosing to love again, and the role the WOW plays in his life and in his heart, lest any WOW be branded forever as nothing more than a substitute for "the real thing", or be forever labeled as "the other woman".

13

DEALING WITH INTERPERSONAL RELATIONSHIPS AS A WOW

Who Will Be My Friend?

WOWs often feel isolated and alone in their situations. It is hard to "whine and kvetch" about insecure feelings relating to a ghost who should pose no real threat without sounding like a selfish, self-centered, insecure femme fatale who has no respect for the dead or for her husband's grief. So the WOW often buries her confusing feelings deep inside for fear of being misunderstood and judged harshly. She feels that neither society nor her own husband will ever come to understand her, so she has no one with whom to discuss, and thereby work out, her WOW issues.

Most second wives of divorced men have the luxury of feeling their husbands are "on their side", and are more willing to listen to their wives' frustrations about the ex-wives, usually because they stand united in their mutual negative feelings about her. Husbands of WOWs often will not listen to his new wife's lamentations because he views her feelings as a betrayal to his precious memories or an insult to the late woman herself. Therefore, he often cannot find it in his heart to comfort his new wife, since doing so would constitute validation of her feelings, putting him in the position of the betrayer.

Death Factors In

It is a fact that society, as a whole, is uncomfortable with death and death-related issues. I know this is true, because I am often faced with funerals at which I stammer over the right thing to say, or *not* to say, to the grief-stricken survivors. I want to show my deepest and most sincerely felt sympathy, but do so in a way that does not cause the survivor any more grief than he or she is already experiencing. Saying something like "I know how you feel" is not only stupid but also untrue, since I have never lost a loved one to death, nor have I lost that *particular* loved one whose funeral I am attending.

And even if I were a survivor myself, it would still be impossible to understand another person's depth of grief.

Death, like everything else, is a part of life, and as such, becomes a reality check. It reminds us that we cannot live forever. Death is only taboo because we can't really control it. It just happens—to everyone at some point. And when it does happen to someone we love, our grief is uniquely separate from anyone else's loss experience.

I suppose all this makes survivors appear to be "unapproachable" because we who are on the outside of their grief fear making matters worse, but also because we *do* feel uncomfortable discussing death. Human beings crave understanding and true empathy when we go through difficult times, and if the people around us can't provide it, we become "unapproachable". So I wonder...are we WOWs also unapproachable because death has touched us *indirectly*? We all deal with certain categories of loneliness—the loneliness of not really fitting in neatly into society. And for WOWs, this pain of isolation is all too common.

My Experiences

For me, it's been difficult in that area of my life. At a time when I was going through the major upheavals of moving to a foreign country, having a relationship with a widower, dealing with children of divorce, while at the same time planning my wedding, I discovered that I had no one around me who was on MY side. I moved into "their" social circle, to friends and family who had been there *intimately* for my husband when his wife died, and I felt like a complete and utter outsider. Even to this day, I don't feel really close to the friends who knew the late wife even though they have been very nice. There's some kind of barrier between us that won't budge, no matter how many times we put on our masks and pretend.

Since moving to my husband's hometown, I have eventually met a few new people who did not know the late wife. Many are mothers, so a lot of our conversation revolves around our children, but I still feel that people define me by my WOW situation when they eventually learn of it. When I mention my husband's past marriage, his late wife, or my issues surrounding both to the people I meet, they politely assure me that they DO understand, but it's simply not true. They WANT to understand, but they haven't got a clue.

Even though they didn't know the late wife, they are fascinated by the position I'm in, and conversation STILL inevitably revolves back to the late wife. I often fantasize about acquiring a circle of wise friends who would be able to empathize with the peculiarities of my life without invoking "her" presence.

Because of the fear that surrounds death, people will innocently and naively say some really dumb things. Even the false pleasantries and misplaced sympathies can leave you feeling lonelier than ever because they demonstrate just how misunderstood your situation really is. Well-meaning folks can even simply offer me a genuine "I'm so sorry", but then I can see the millions of questions rolling around in their heads. It's like nobody knows how to "handle" me. I find myself keeping things to myself more and more and sticking to "safe" topics.

I suppose the only way to not be placed in a category, and therefore defined by it, is to not let anyone be privy to my unique situation. But that is nearly impossible because society loves its labels, and tries to place people in some kind of category so that they *can* relate.

Human Nature Interferes

I doubt that I am defensive around people—I just think I'm afraid of all the nonsensical platitudes I might get, like all of those things people say when they're *trying* to get it. It's more a feeling that no matter how hard I try to explain how I feel, preconceived notions are always just that bit stronger, putting me more into a defensive position—one that I loathe.

I don't believe that non-WOW behavior is necessarily right or wrong, though. Neither is my loneliness or the perception that I am not approachable all their fault, either. I think many times human beings just need to vent and want someone just to listen, but the kind-hearted listeners who simply cannot relate will care enough to give advice and generally want to *FIX* the problem. They feel that if they keep silent, the person sharing with them will think they don't care. In other words, better to say something stupid than nothing at all.

In a friendship, you need to be able to take some information for granted, and that's very difficult to do when your experiences are so very different from those around you. Explaining every little WOW nuance is almost impossible, and misunderstandings abound. Mind you, I'll keep trying, but I've become a lot more aware of the challenges of creating a social circle in a second marriage when there's been an untimely and tragic death. When you open up to someone and show your soft underbelly, you need expert handling by someone who can "look inside you" without judgment. Those people are hard to come by when you're a WOW.

"Their" Friends

My husband's circle of friends is sometimes an uncomfortable reminder to me that he was married before and I am the second wife. His friends, in turn, sometimes cannot get past that uncomfortable feeling of wishing I were "her" and that they were still having all that "fun" together that they used to have, along with all those great memories of my husband and his late wife. They like me and try to be friends, but "she" will always come up somewhere in the conversation pertaining to something they did together or something they miss about "her". It hurts just listening to them walk down memory lane, but I also fear that I may never be able to trust them to really *know* ME!

We WOWs are also a constant reminder that a husband can go on to be very happy after the death of a wife. We also shatter the image of every couple getting the chance to grow old together. I think that makes a lot of people really uncomfortable, because we break the illusion of one man for each woman for all eternity.

Friends from "their" past may fear that their relationship with the widower will never be the same again, or as good as it was when the late wife was still a part of their lives. They may fear being left out, thinking that perhaps the WOW will want no part of them because of their ties to the past. They may feel uncomfortable around the WOW because it is hard for them to picture the widower with anyone else but their dearly departed friend. They may judge the WOW harshly, feeling that she pales in comparison to their wonderful friend. Sadly, they may never give the WOW the chance she deserves to mend the broken circle.

Friends may fear that the WOW's presence in the widower's life will erase the late wife's memory completely from his heart, and that the WOW will somehow facilitate this and use it to her own advantage, perhaps by breaking ties with them. They may hold the WOW in contempt for "replacing" their late friend, or dislike her just because she is a totally unique and different woman than the late wife was. And they may feel bereavement all over again as they stand by, helplessly watching the late wife's husband make dramatic changes in his life by remarrying someone else.

What Can We Do?

As WOWs, we have to appear to be larger than life. We have to believe in our marriages, our choices, our "present wife" roles, and ourselves more than ever. We must present ourselves to the world as capable women with strong, confident exteriors in order to survive in these situations of ours, even if doing so goes against some of our truly negative WOW feelings, copping a sort of "fake it 'til you make it" kind of attitude.

Either that, or we must find a way to make people understand, to educate them as to the "right" and "wrong" ways to have a close relationship with a WOW, in order that they can better understand us and therefore, empathize. But finding a way to do this takes time and practice, as well as people on both sides of the issues that are willing to participate in reaching a better understanding.

To that end, I have compiled a list of helpful tips for the non-WOW that will help with understanding and befriending a WOW:

Please, Do NOT...:

...say anything about the late wife unless I initiate it. *(If I do start a discussion about the late wife, please follow my lead and refrain from referring to her as "his first wife" or "his wife".)*

...ask questions about my husband's grief. *(I can barely grasp it myself.)*

...go into detail about the losses that YOU have experienced and how you dealt with them. *(We are two different people dealing with entirely different issues.)*

...trivialize my husband's grief by saying, "God has a plan for everything", or, "God needed her more up in Heaven than your husband did here on earth", or, "God never gives us more than we can bear", and do NOT ask me if the late wife "Made her peace with God" before she died. *(I wasn't there, so I don't know. I love the Lord, but I'm not a minister, and neither are you, so how can you speak for God?)*

...try to amuse me with unasked-for stories about the late wife, if you knew her. *(I am not amused.)*

...ask me where she is buried, or if my husband has an adjoining plot for his future use. *(I am hoping I never have to see him use it, and if and when I do, I want him next to his wife—me!)*

...ask me if my husband or I still feel(s) her presence. *(If I wanted ghosts, I would've married either a psychic or an exorcist.)*

...tell me what you would do or how you would feel if you were in my shoes. *(You have no idea until or unless you marry a widower, so you cannot properly advise me.)*

...analyze me by telling me "It's all in your (my) head". *(I am not crazy. I am human.)*

Please Don't Say Something Stupid, Like:

"I knew the late wife, and you're nothing like her." *(Great! I gotta be me! But you're probably wondering how my husband could've married someone so different? Please, don't compare me, even if your statement was meant as a compliment.)*

"I knew the late wife, and you're so much like her!" *(But I'm NOT her!...and thank God my husband recognizes the difference.)*

"Well, now he can forget her (the late wife) since he married you." *(He'll never "forget" her, and I wouldn't wish that for him, anyway.)*

"He may never feel for you like he did her, but at least you can make him as happy as he CAN be for now." *(I wouldn't have married him if I knew that he couldn't possibly love me the way he loved her...or better. Besides that, she and I are two different people, and you cannot love two separate people the same way.)*

"I know how you feel" or "I understand your pain" or "I can relate". *(You don't, and you can't.)*

"You're lucky! I wish MY ex was dead!" *(She's NOT an "ex"...she's a "why?")*

"I married a divorced man, so I can relate!" *(No, you can't...it's two completely different sets of issues.)*

"I'm so happy that he now has a mother for his children". *(That's not why he married me, and I am not replacing the children's real mother.)*

"Oh, so you like camping (or whatever)? Oh, she did, too!" *(Oh, what a coincidence! Must be why he married me—to clone her.)*

"It's been two weeks/six months/three years! How long are you going to let this control your life?" or, "She's gone—just get over it" or ""Life is for the living! Don't worry your life away over a dead woman. It's time you moved on". *(If it were that easy, I'd have "been there" or "done that" by now.)*

"Why don't you do something positive with your life that will distract you?" *(Nothing and no one will ever make me forget. I have too many reminders in my daily life and marriage, thank you.)*

"I haven't come over, because as long as I don't, I can pretend that she's still there." *(Then you won't mind if I pretend that you're not saying something that stupid?)*

"You seem to be taking this well." *(You wouldn't want to see me when I am upset.)*

"You should be settled in by now." *(Adjusting to my role as a WOW is not something one "settles" into…it's one I grow from.)*

"So, how do your husband's family (or former in-laws) feel about his remarrying?" *(If you really want to know, ask them.)*

"I really miss her (the late wife)". *(My husband does, too, and that's why I need some sympathy.)*

"I'm sure she (the late wife) would approve of you." *(I don't need her approval, and neither did/does my husband.)*

"She's probably watching over your husband from heaven right now." *(Egads, that's ALL I need! Besides, how do YOU know she's looking down instead of up?)*

"What's it like raising another woman's child(ren)?" *(He/She/They is/are mine now, or at least that's how it feels.)*

"How nice that you gave him the child she couldn't." *(My husband and I created OUR child. I was not the late wife's surrogate.)*

"Well, at least he's not alone anymore." *(He didn't marry me because he was lonely. He married me because he loved me.)*

"I'm sure you must understand why her family can't accept you." *(No, I can't. And if you can't explain it to me, don't opine about it!)*

"She was a wonderful person…but I'm sure you are, too." *(You don't know me, so you can't compare us.)*

Well, at least she's not around to make your life miserable like an ex would." *(She's still around, in her own way…and that's why I need a hug.)*

Please DO…:

…start any questions with, "How does it feel…?" or "How do you feel…?" *(It's nice to know you care about my feelings, opinions, and perspective.)*

…feel free to tell me how you think I am a good wife for my husband. *(But only if it has nothing to do with "rescuing" him from his grief or his prior widower status.)*

…treat me like you would anyone else. *(Because I am!)*

…acknowledge my feelings without judgment. *(If you can't relate, you can't be judgmental.)*

…tell me I am doing all the right things to make my husband happy. *(It's why I wanted to be his wife.)*

…congratulate my husband and me, and wish us well in our future together. *(We're trying as hard as we can to live for the present.)*

…get angry *with* me when I rage about the unfairness of non-acceptance. *(Misery loves company!)*

…tell me about the late wife ONLY when I ask. *(But please, don't make her sound saintly, and only answer the question I ask. Don't go on and on about her.)*

Please DO say something wonderful, like…:

…"I can see why your husband loves you." *(You, my dear, will get a Valentine's Day card from me!)*

…"I'm so glad you're going to be part of our circle of friends." *(I want to belong, as long as you accept me for me, and not because I am "filling in for" the late wife in the group.)*

…"It MUST be hard for you, I can't even imagine!" *(You can't, but I appreciate your eagerness to learn about me, as well as your willingness to validate that my feelings are real to me.)*

…"You don't have to talk about her if you don't want to, but if you do, I'll listen." *(I appreciate that more than you know.)*

…"You're his wife now, and that's what counts." *(That's so true!)*

…"I didn't know her, but I'd like to get to know you." *(Thank you for putting the past where it belongs.)*

…"Hey, you wanna go get a cup of coffee with me and chat?" *(You like me! You really LIKE me!)*

…"I can't relate, but I feel badly that you feel badly." *(You're my new best friend!)*

14

WOW BOUNDARIES: THE LINES IN THE SAND

Setting Comfort Zones

Remember the old "Our Gang" series on television? I remember one episode in which Spanky draws a line in the dirt with his toe, and dares his archenemy to cross it. He had his arms crossed, his jutted chin firmly planted in the air, and his brows furrowed, with a menacing sneer on his face. He may actually have been scared to death, worrying that he may actually have to deliver on his threat, but his face belied his fears. I don't remember the ending, but I can't get that mental picture of Spanky's face out of my head to this day! It was one that beguiled his otherwise charming and sweet personality.

I believe we WOWs need to draw a similar imaginary line in the sand when it comes to our own personal boundaries. A boundary is, by definition, something (like a line, point, or plane) that indicates or fixes a limit or extent. We need to let the people in our lives know the extent or limit of what we can tolerate and what we cannot when it comes to our issues where the late wife is concerned. And, if the line is crossed, we also need to stand our ground, chins firmly planted in the air and, no matter how scared we are, and effectively "beat down the bully" who defies us, even when doing so demonstrates the polar opposite of our normally sweet and charming selves.

Don't get me wrong—I am not advocating violence here! I just believe there are times in our lives when we must tactfully but firmly adjust someone's preconceived notions and attitude towards WOWs by either setting the record straight, voicing our displeasure, or tuning them in as to how we expect to be treated.

We do the same for our children, although we usually call it "discipline". Child experts claim that disciplining a child should not be about punishment, but about *education*. We, as parents, must make rules and expect them to be obeyed. We must set limits and expect them to be respected. When they are not, the child learns through our displeasure, and the consequences we implement, that they have done something wrong, and to never do it again.

So, too, must we allow people the opportunity to grow and learn by educating them as to their errors, however innocent, when they have crossed the line of our WOW boundaries, even enforcing the lesson with consequences for their actions.

Michelle's Story

For example, my WOW friend "Michelle" complained how she felt angry that, after 7 years, her sister-in-law still kept referring to her as "Sharon", her husband's late wife.

While I believe the sister-in-law's slip of the tongue was most likely just an innocent faux pas based on an old habit, Michelle drew the line in the sand, and had a serious talk with her. She calmly but firmly said,

> *"Sis, I notice that you always refer to me as "Sharon", and I have to tell you—I really hate it. It makes me feel like you don't accept me as your brother's new wife. I understand that you probably don't even realize you are doing it, but it hurts, and I'd like you to please stop it. And if you can't, then I really don't think I'd feel comfortable coming over to your house any more, and I'd really miss that."*

"Sis" was shocked. She related to Michelle that she had no idea she was not using Michelle's name, and that she was glad Michelle had brought the problem to her attention. She even went so far as to suggest that Michelle do something—like tap her on the shoulder—if she ever made that mistake again. It's been three years since Michelle had this discussion with her sister-in-law, and she has only had to tap sister-in-law once after that.

I think this is an excellent example of how to go about setting your WOW boundaries with grace. When we take a closer look at Michelle's plea to her sister-in-law, we see that she first stated the problem, and then related how it made her feel. She then offered understanding and/or an "easy out" for her sister-in-law. After this, she then drew the line in the sand by stating what she wanted and how she expected to be treated in the future. And finally, she enforced the lesson with consequences that she was prepared to undertake. While some people may perceive Michelle's stance as "bitchy", that is the risk we WOWs must be willing to take in order to gain new understanding and respect for our positions and our feelings.

Boundaries For Him

Most of the time, it is only the "outsiders" who force us to set personal limits. They don't know our situations and us well enough yet, if at all, to comprehend our feelings. But sometimes, our own family members, as in Michelle's case, can innocently (or not so innocently) inflict unintentional (or intentional) pain on the WOW simply because they take too much for granted, or they *think* they understand the WOW without really knowing her intimately enough. Even previously widowed husbands of WOWs can screw up, sometimes without even realizing it.

I believe it is of paramount importance to a widower and to his second marriage that he learns to be empathetic about, and tuned into, his wife's WOW issues and her needs relating to them. And, fortunately, most are, if we have done our jobs as WOWs and discussed our issues with our husbands frequently. But man is human, and sometimes does not see the forest for the trees.

To illustrate: My WOW friend "Barbara's" husband was and is a great support for her in dealing with her WOW issues. If she has had a problem with one of her WOW insecurities, her husband has been quick to reaffirm his love for her and work with her towards a solution or compromise.

However, her husband has a bad habit of sometimes comparing sex with Barbara to sex with his late wife. Sex is such a sensitive issue for anyone anyway, but for a WOW, it is even that much more. We fear comparisons that might not be favorable, causing us to become intimidated in the bedroom, thus creating a total break down of communicating our sexual needs.

Barbara confided,

> *"My husband is a great lover. He is not at all selfish in bed. On the contrary, he is very generous in pleasing me, and he enjoys my excitement and response to him. But sometimes he will touch me in a way that I don't like, and I will gently tell him so. Then, he will get a perplexed look on his face and say, 'Gee, I don't get it. "Sally" (his late wife) used to love it!'"*

By relating his bewilderment to Barbara in such a way, her husband had sparked Barbara's WOW insecurity and invited the "ghost" into their bed. Perhaps her husband's comments were innocent enough in that he may just truly believe that all women are the same, sexually speaking; therefore, all must enjoy the same sexual touches, foreplay, and positions. But his ignorance does not excuse his comparison to his late wife in Barbara's presence while in their marital bed.

I advised Barbara to open up a dialogue with her husband by setting her boundary, and explained how my WOW friend "Michelle" had handled a similar problem with her own sister-in-law recently. So Barbara sat down with her husband, and said,

> *"I have a problem with your comparing me to your late wife, sexually. I am hurt when you tell me that "Sally" liked to be touched in a way that I do not. I am not Sally—I am me. You must understand that different women have different sexual needs unique to them, so please don't make me feel sexually inadequate or unusual by comparing me to her again, or I may lose interest in making love with you, although I would miss that very much."*

Barbara's husband comforted her by admitting that he wasn't aware of the depth of her pain, and he would never again speak of his late wife's sexuality.

Both of these friends of mine stood their ground, and were rewarded for their determination to forge a new understanding with the people they loved. They demanded respect for their feelings, and they earned it. Their method of drawing lines was not at all "bitchy", but tactful, graceful, loving, and compassionate, while at the same time firm, direct, and serious. And, in all cases, necessary.

When To Speak Up, and When To Be Still

But is there ever a time when setting your personal WOW boundaries is not necessary? Are there times when demanding respect for your boundaries is just a plea for sympathy or a cry for help? For instance, have you ever berated someone because of a casual mention of the late wife?

I recall one instance early in my marriage when I took someone to task for such a reason. My WOW insecurities were new and therefore, raw. I had built a defensive wall around me, feeling suspicious of anyone who knew the late wife. A woman had just been introduced to me at a social function in her home, and she smiled and said, *"Nice to meet you. I knew your husband's late wife, but I want you to feel welcome."* Much to my husband's embarrassment, and everyone else's amazement, I let her have it, saying in a rather loud voice, *"I'm NOT her! And I don't want to hear about her!"* There is no way that this fine lady deserved my wrath, but it was my way of drawing attention to my plight and hoping to garner sympathy, albeit in a juvenile and tactless way.

Not everyone you meet will have a hidden agenda or a secret desire to hurt you just because of your label of "WOW". Some are just plain curious. Some will say ridiculous things just because they are ignorant as to your unique position. These people and their remarks are forgivable, and we can overlook their innocent enough blunders and take them with a grain of salt if we remember to save our most important boundary-setting for the people in our lives who really care and whom we really care about, while also remembering to do so with a grace that leads to a better understanding.

15

BEATING THE ODDS

When I was researching grief information prior to marrying my previously widowed husband, I was dismayed by the statistics I discovered. As I recall, one Ivy League university study showed that the second (and other subsequent) marriages of widowed people lasted an average of *only 3 years!*

But why? I looked further, and found no individual statistical analysis for each participant involved in the study. In other words, no reasons were given as to why the parties involved (the widowed and their spouses) failed to make it to their fourth anniversary, based *solely* on the fact that one half of each marital union was previously widowed!

Even some religious leaders in major organized faiths, I discovered, have gone so far as to counsel widows and widowers themselves not to remarry but to remain faithful to their deceased spouses and honor their memory. Well, we've come a long way from that narrowly defined advice, thank goodness! Still, here I was, about to become a blushing bride, feeling that some cold, hard data was telling me that my marriage was not only doomed to fail, but that our wedding vows should never be spoken in the first place!

I truly believe in pre-marital counseling of any sort, no matter what the future spouse's background may have been. In fact, in some churches, it is a requirement of pre-marriage. A prior marriage, even when successful, does not replace the need for a thorough evaluation and preparation for remarriage, especially for widowers and WOWs. We deserve a full, meaningful preparation that recognizes and is responsive to our special needs. While the grief process may be the most obvious issue that would affect the success of a widower/WOW marriage, other issues related to step parenting, blended families, financial and property arrangements, and other concerns should receive careful consideration in marriage preparation.

It is true that the widower status of one's future spouse carries with it a certain amount of "baggage" that needs to be and should be addressed, as marriage to a widower is a uniquely complicated situation. However, I am loathe to believe that the death of one's former spouse automatically and statistically nullifies the success of any future marriage, and I refuse to accept that a widower enters remarriage not with his eyes wide open, but with the pieces of his broken heart in his hands, giving his future bride her only purpose for their marriage—to mend it!

Sure Could Use Some Good News!

Another study I discovered focused on remarriage patterns of those recently widowed, and said that the death of a spouse causes the economic and physical health of the surviving spouse to decline. The authors of this study felt that remarriage is one way to reduce this decline.

And in numerous other articles I researched, authors and educators alike felt that, generally speaking, men would tend to want to remarry to find a companion as a replacement, being unable to deal with loneliness, and that there also appears to be a sexual aspect to men finding it more urgent to remarry.

OK, so let me get this straight. My previously widowed husband wants to marry me because he's lonely, financially unstable, in poor physical health, wants a replacement wife, has an uncontrollable sexual appetite that needs whetting, and we're doomed to a three year marriage? I wanted to run screaming into the streets! This seemed so unfair! But I diligently persevered, and discovered that while there appears to be a handful of "factoids" that, on the surface, support the studies and noted scholars, there is plenty of opposing and more hopeful data.

So, I came to the conclusion that: A.) Mom was right—don't believe everything you read, and B.) The fact is most remarriage failure has little to do with any given spouse's prior marital status and more to do with the maturity (or immaturity) of each partner, *regardless* of prior status!

Debunking The Myth

In an effort to debunk the myth that widower remarriages will never last a life-time, and that widowers only remarry for shallow, selfish, and unsubstantiated reasons, I want to share with you some enlightening and uplifting information I have found which validates what I have felt to be true all along…that the real tests of any remarriage—maturity and commitment—hold true for widowers as well.

In her article, "Why Many Say 'I Do' Again", Dr. Eleanor Hamilton, a retired psychologist, sex therapist, and the author of five books, tells us about the remarriage of mature men:

> "…Men who have developed resiliency and flexibility in their lives have a distinct advantage over men who had led conventionally restrained lives."

> "Resilient men have already had long experience in accepting challenges and trying out new solutions to problems. After a period of grieving the death of a beloved wife, they may plunge themselves into some new and absorbing activity. Or they may devote themselves to a pursuit they have always dreamed of but couldn't indulge in while young and carrying the responsibilities of a young family. For a while these resilient and resourceful men may keep themselves feeling alive and vital as they go about their new enterprises. But the time soon comes when they long for the intimacies that they realize will exist for them only in a marriage or a committed relationship."

It would appear that Dr. Hamilton agrees with the notion that "what doesn't kill you makes you stronger", and that widowers bring with them into remarriage a strength unmatched by mere data. Not only that, but we can conclude it has been Dr. Hamilton's experience that widowers need the commitment that marriage brings in order to feel complete and whole.

In "Finishing Touches: Survivor Choices After the Death of a Spouse", Lillian Hawthorne, a widow, retired clinical practitioner and university professor in the field of social work in Camarillo, California writes,

"...Widowers do not really want to remain alone. Indeed, most of us, no matter our age or condition, want to share our lives with someone else. Especially having once known the experience of a life partner, we know how important, even though sometimes imperfect, such a relationship can be."

"It is not so much major events or exciting experiences we want to share with someone because if truth be told, there are not many of these in our older lives but simply our daily doings. We want to have someone to tell about what we did each day, whom we saw or spoke to, what we bought, even what we ate. We want someone to do things with even if there is nothing specific or special we want to do. We want to have somebody nearby to worry about us, to help us if something goes wrong, or just to be there to know when or if something goes wrong. In fact, one of the greatest fears of living alone is that something may happen to us and there will be nobody to know about it. Sharing with a friend, no matter how likable or sympathetic, is only a necessary, but inadequate, substitute. Even the most caring friends have other friends who occupy similar relationships with them; they cannot be specially and uniquely with us or for us."

Ms. Hawthorne appears to be telling us that widowers know what makes a good wife and a strong marriage, they miss it, and they want it for themselves again, thereby demystifying the clinical analysis that says widowers are helpless in deciding what they really want because they are so hopelessly immobilized by grief.

Susan Shapiro Barash, in her book, "Second Wives: The Pitfalls and Rewards Of Marrying Widowers and Divorced Men", writes this about widowers and remarriage:

"The husband comes to his second wife with a sense of the world and of what can happen in life. If he has been widowed, he knows how precious the days are and how quickly happiness can evaporate. He looks to his second wife with the knowledge of what he wants and how to live out the second half. She benefits greatly, because there will be no fits and starts, but her husband's maturity will guide them smoothly in life decision."

"The second wife is the second chance for her husband. Second wives should never forget that whatever the difficulties, however insurmountable they seem, they, as second wives, offer their husbands hope and happiness. The second wife brings security and love for the second half, the second go round."

With all that going for him, how can a widower's remarriage be so doomed for failure? Simply put—it doesn't have to be!

I personally feel that the media has heaped an unnecessary burden on the widower by consistently pointing out the negative aspects of his life-altering experience instead of mentioning some of the benefits—those that will help him heal and allow him to function more positively as a husband the second time around, which in turn benefit the WOW in many positive ways.

16

THE WIDOWER'S TURN

I truly believe that the only way to empathize compassionately is to picture yourself in the other person's shoes and walk around in them for a while while trying to get an idea of what that person may be feeling. This is no easy task when you try this scenario with a widower.

Most women I know find it nearly impossible to gauge what the male of the species thinks or feels at any given time (and I'm sure that most men would safely assume the same about most women!). Therefore, it is for this reason that I find it hard to fathom what a variety of widowers is feeling when I first meet them, coupled with the fact that each man grieves in his own way and in different stages. It has been said that no one ever truly comprehends grief unless or until it happens to them personally, so it would follow that since I have never lost a spouse, I cannot try on a widower's shoes comfortably.

So how DOES a prospective WOW find the answer to the question, *"What do widowers want?"*

Accept Me As I Am

I'd like to think that widowers want from a new wife basically what any man would want, but I know that is too simplistic, given all that a widower has been through in his life. Do a widower's wants and needs in a relationship change just because he lost his first wife? Frankly—yes!

If life is an "evolutionary" process, then everyone's life experiences help each person to change and grow. Widowers are no exception. Sometimes one must endure certain experiences in one's past before appreciating what one has in the present. Losing a wife through death forever changes a widower's perception of life and of himself.

The following is a beautiful insight from the husband of my WOW friend, "Cathy":

> *"When my late wife died, a big part of the "me" I was while married to her died, too. I had to heal and re-build myself and who I was, and I had to learn how to live and how to feel again. Looking back, I know that I am a very different person than I was before she died. I was not as introspective, as sensitive, as expressive, or as loving as I am today. I have very different interests, different attitudes, and different priorities. Her dying changed me forever…and I feel very guilty for saying this, but if by some miracle she came back today, she would not be the person that I would choose to be with…my present wife is, because we are better suited for each other based on our past life experiences."*

Cathy responds to her husband's words this way:

> *"Ironically, this change "caused" by his late wife led him to evolve away from her—after all, she herself and the memory of her are frozen in time because of her death."*

Widowers are survivors, and as such, most come through the grief process much stronger, more resilient, and embrace life with more gusto. Those are big changes for any person, but it would appear that for the widower, this growth is marked not by the passage of time but by how he handles the cards that are dealt to him.

In my marriage, I find that my husband is much more patient with my WOW issues than he used to be, but when that patience thins, the bottom line is that he wants me to just "get over it" and "move on". I believe that what this translates to is, *"Believe that I love you and stop trying to make me prove it over and over again just to reassure you"*. The widower wants his new wife to accept the baggage that he brought into the relationship, but not be controlled by it. He wants his wife to be able to accept him as he is—a man who happens to be a widower—just as we hope he will accept *her* for all that she is as a woman and for what she brings into the marriage from her past.

Truth be told, most widowers hope that their wives will move on in the same way and into the same cerebral place as they have. They don't want their wives to be insecure. They don't want to agonize over hearing us comparing ourselves to the late wife. They don't want us to view the late wife as "the enemy" or feel threatened by her. They want a loving relationship—not with a ghost, not with a substitution or replacement or clone, but with US—in the "here and now".

Whatever the circumstances that led to him being who he is today, even if it meant he loved someone else before us truly, madly, and deeply, a widower basically wants from the WOW her love and acceptance of the man he is—and the man he has become.

A Good "Catch"

WOWs are lucky women to be married to men who know how to make a marriage work and have proven records of commitment, and WOWs are also fortunate to be married to men who can love with all their hearts because they know from experience that there IS a beautiful rainbow after every dark storm.

On the plus side, you are dealing with a man who has learned the hard way to embrace life, appreciate all it offers, and live it to the fullest, since he knows that life can be short and that time is fleeting. In his eyes, he had the best, and he won't settle for anything less the second time around, either! Consider yourself complimented!

I believe that because my husband lost a wife prior to marrying me, he was changed by the whole experience in many distinct ways. I think that he has learned to be more sacrificing, more appreciative of what he has, and definitely more caring and less selfish. He is also more acutely sensitive to his family's needs, and has a more profound sense of what "family" is really all about. The experience has taught him that life is short and cannot be taken for granted.

Had he not endured this great loss, perhaps he would be much less introspective, less empathic, less tender, and much more limited in every direction of his emotional spectrum. But now, he has this unbelievably mature perspective that life is all about change, and change equals growth. It's an ironic truth in life that growth and love come from great pain and tragedy. In other words, how do we define "sweet" if we have never tasted "sour"? Who better than a widower to model this?

Perhaps I would not have been attracted to my husband as the person he was before his late wife passed away, considering how much he HAS grown and changed because of the loss. If the old adage *"All things, good and bad, happen for a reason"* is true, then perhaps in order for him to be the perfect match for me, he first had to evolve into the man I fell in love with. And to do that, he had to go through all the life experiences…the good, the bad, and the ugly…that made him who he is today.

I am often asked if part of my romantic interest in, or attraction to, my husband was related to the fact that he was indeed a widower. Well, perhaps it did—indirectly. It **did** cause me to be more empathetic early in our relationship, which encouraged our budding friendship to blossom into love. But more often than not, the hidden meaning behind the question is, did I feel that I had something to gain, emotionally speaking, from his prior marital status?

Allow me to illustrate. My husband's late wife died of cancer a year after her diagnosis. And for a good part of that year prior to her eventual and inevitable death, he was her caretaker. Hollywood enjoys romanticizing this supreme sacrifice by portraying the selfless widower-to-be in movies as his dying spouse's hero. His nurturing her until her last breath in his arms is both moving and touching, epic in its surrealism and in the emotional payoff at the box office. In reality, my husband did what he felt was appropriate and right as his wife's husband. He took his "for better or worse, in sickness and in health" marriage vows very seriously. In short, he did what needed to be done, but he did so out of love—not to be a hero—one day at a time.

A widower who was his late wife's caretaker is more often than not a man who has seen the ugly side of life, and still finds life beautiful. He knows what inner strength is all about, has had his resolved tested, and has passed with flying colors. He stands as a true symbol of commitment, for he is honorable in having respected the meaning of his marital vows. He knows there is no obstacle that love and faith cannot overcome, as he makes his way through the valley of the shadow of death and into the light.

Do I, as a WOW, have something to gain from this? Absolutely! Did I plan it this way? Of course not...and neither did he. Life happens...for a reason. And those reasons are beneficial to both of you in your marriage because they are what build character.

People sometimes ask me, *"Would you marry a widower again, knowing what you know now about being a WOW?"* I always respond positively. The love I share and the life I make with my husband are bigger, stronger, and more important than my WOW label or his widower status. Those are categories that society uses to pigeonhole us, but he and I will not allow ourselves to be defined as such. We are, simply, a married couple, comprised of two individuals with unique life experiences.

Like any other life situation, you can CHOOSE to make your WOW experience either a positive one or a hellish nightmare, depending upon on how you handle the tough WOW issues. Look at your husband and ask yourself, "Is he worth it?" I'm willing to bet your answer is a resounding "YES!"

Expect Your Marriage To Be a Happy One!!

When all your WOW fears, doubts, and insecurities have been calmed with honest and open communication with your husband, when you learn about grief and its components, when you have set in motion the compromises and boundaries that you can live with, and when you come to accept your husband's late wife into your life in a way that you do not resent, then life with a widower and your marriage to one will be full of wonderful, joyful experiences for both of you. You have the rest of your lives to make your own memories, set your own priorities, and be respectful and compassionate partners to each other.

Most WOWs I have met or communicated with in my lifetime have always appeared to me to be the kindest, sweetest, most understanding, patient, and caring women I have ever known. And now, being married to a widower, I can see why they necessarily have to be!

There is a spark in their marriages that is to be envied. There is a kind reverence...a warm, gentle knowledge that life is precious and fragile, and should be lived with awe and wonder, excitement and joy, with more than enough love to last a lifetime. Life after loss CAN be wonderful if you are both willing to work at it.

In every widower's heart, there are deeply imbedded seeds—those of endurance, of resiliency, and of an understanding that love can be, to borrow from an old song, "more beautiful the second time around". This is his gift to you as his wife, his WOW...and wow, are you a lucky woman!

What My Widowed Husband Has Taught Me

When two people become one flesh by way of marriage, it is not only their hearts that are united, but their minds and souls as well. Intertwined in unison, this melding of two spirits gives rise to a new way of looking at the world, for it is no longer just your own heart that feels, but your spouse's as well. His pain becomes your pain; his joy becomes your joy...and vice versa. And along this marital road to discovering each other, your spouse's traits that you have learned to love, admire, accept, appreciate, nurture, and respect, become your own personal goals as well.

Before I met my previously widowed husband, I lacked experience in, and knowledge about, issues such as death, dying, and grief. All I possessed were some basic beliefs about each, but nothing tangible upon which to base them. My husband, however, had cornered the market on all three, sadly enough. Not only had he lost his terminally ill first wife of seven years, but his past also harbored the losses of a dearly beloved father and a brother. I'm sure we'd all agree that he has endured the greatest tragedies one can ever humanly experience.

But we who lack experience can only speculate how we would handle such occurrences if and when death touches out lives, either directly or indirectly. Yes, we would be heartbroken...our lives shattered and upended...but would we survive, perhaps even thrive, because of them? Via the example set by my husband, and the wisdom he has shared with me, I have learned some valuable insights into this thing called grief and its effects on the lives of its survivors. Through the years of being truly "as one" with him, I have absorbed my husband's character into my own, and now see things not only through more compassionate eyes, but more hopeful and wiser ones as well.

The following are my tender observations and life lessons gleaned from loving a man who has endured tragic loss, and yet has found his way out of the darkness of grief into the light of life anew. They are the reasons why I love my husband eternally, and they are also the inspiration for the best changes I have ever made to my outlook on life. Though they may sound like platitudes or clichés, when learned along the journey of grief or by loving someone who walks this journey daily, they tend to take on a whole new meaning for everyday life and become words to live by:

All things happen for a reason—even if you have no idea what that reason is at the time.

After my husband lost his first wife, a minister quoted this line to him in great earnest and sympathy. Thank God he was a man of the cloth, or my husband probably would have pounded him into salt, for the last thing a newly bereaved spouse needs or wants to hear is that their dearly departed was taken from this earth "for a reason". To them, there is no earthly excuse for a loving God to take away a life partner, thereby causing the survivors so much anguish.

Years later, however, my husband came to realize that these words were true. He now, after all these years, possesses the wisdom of hindsight, and has surmised that perhaps his wife died for reasons he cannot and may never fully understand, but are within the perfect will of the Almighty. Having such a tragedy deepen his faith has only served to comfort him when faced with other dark times in his life.

I have learned that there is much peace to be found in accepting that a Higher Power with greater plans for our lives than we can ever fathom—as well as a love that is bigger than we could ever imagine—allows bad things to happen to us so that we might pass the tests of faith, grow, learn, and yes, even prosper because of them.

Life is a choice—as is how you handle the pitfalls along its bumpy road.

"You can be better or bitter—the choice is up to you". I have heard these pearls of sage advice from my mother echo in my mind many times when I have experienced devastating blows in my life. But I never really accepted them until I met my widowed husband.

There is something attractive about a man who faces life's challenges with a positive outlook, and often, this perception is forged from great loss. My husband *chose* to live a positive, productive life after the death of his first wife. He could have remained a bitter, angry survivor, stuck in a rut of self-pity. And while no one could have blamed him should he have chosen this path, it would not have served him well. He made a decision to focus on the positive aspects of the life he now faced, and spent productive time nurturing those seeds until they rooted in his character.

I have learned that life is what you make of it. The power and control of all things, good and bad, lies in how you *choose* to mold the outcomes of each life situation. There are many things in life that are beyond our control. But there are few things in life that are beyond our power of choice and our ability to make lemonade from lemons if we just put our minds to it while we focus on the gifts of the present

You're stronger than you think you are.

As my husband's late wife was dying of cancer, he often thought of how he would cope with her eventual death when it finally happened. At the time, he wasn't sure he would survive it. His dark thoughts of making funeral and burial plans for the love of his life were soon realized, however, and although he numbly attended to the details of her passing and the emotional carnage of her loss, he did survive. He often tells me that in retrospect, it surprised him how much stronger he actually was in spite of his prior thoughts of how weak and unable to handle the grief he might be.

"What doesn't kill you makes you stronger". I'm not sure who first quoted these infamous words of wisdom, but whoever it was, he/she was correct. Remember how nervous and insecure you felt the first time you ever gave a speech? Or delivered your first baby? Or went on your first date? You may have thought you'd just die. But you got through all of these scenarios with courage. The next time you spoke to a crowd, or birthed a baby, or took the homecoming queen out to dinner, you weren't as afraid. You had slain the dragons of fear the first time, and danced in their ashes the next. And the next, and so on, until your newfound inner strength became your shield.

I have learned that coping with fear is a challenge for which I welcome. It only means that I will become a stronger, more capable person. Giving into fear, and forever allowing it to paralyze you, is the antithesis of growth.

Accept what you cannot change.

For my husband, the diagnosis of his late wife's terminal cancer was not something he wanted to accept. He delved into reading all he could learn about this dreaded disease in the hope of finding a miracle cure, perhaps something that his late wife's doctors had not yet thought of. He tells me that he wasted precious time—time he could have been enjoying with his late wife, making the most and the best of her final days—as he desperately searched for something...anything...that would change the inevitable.

Had he accepted the doctors' grim but verifiable declarations that they had exhausted all means available to reverse her cancer or keep it from killing her, my husband might not have felt so guilty about using up the last hours of his late wife's life with meticulous and unrelenting research. Instead, he may have been able to cope much easier, and may have been able to ferret out the sweet memories from the horrific, leaving him less prone to guilt.

Hope is a beautiful thing. It gives us peace and strength, and keeps us going when all seems lost. Accepting what you cannot change doesn't mean you have given up on hope. It just means you have to focus your hope on more humanly tangible and attainable goals. It might even mean that you must refocus your hope onto yourself, knowing that whatever the outcome, you will be fine.

I have learned that by accepting what I cannot change, I can embrace the "here and now", live for the moment, and focus on what IS possible, not on what is not.

Endurance and perseverance happen one day at a time.

Every 12-step addiction recovery program teaches its members that they must cope with their addictions one day at a time. Grief recovery program leaders also believe this is the gospel of dealing with grief. Sometimes, especially when you are knee-deep in grief, a day can feel like an eternity. But time is a healer. Days soon turn into weeks, weeks into months, months into years. And as time becomes more of a friend than an enemy, you will look back and be proud of the fact that you have persevered and endured far better than you originally thought possible.

There is no one stronger than one who *has* to be strong, or one who *chooses* to be strong. Surviving one dark day makes you hopeful for that the next one won't be as cloudy. Surviving a year of dark days makes you more and more confident that you have endured and will continue to endure. A lifetime of surviving dark days teaches you perseverance.

I have learned that if I am called upon to endure, I just have to get beyond *today* to make this happen!

Life is for the living—live it with gusto!

No one knows better than bereaved spouses just how precious and fragile life is, for it is they who have watched it slip away from their grasp. Losing a spouse through death has a tendency to make a survivor appreciate his or her own life—and the lives of those he or she loves—more deeply and intimately than ever before.

My husband does not take life for granted any longer. He has learned the hard way that it can be taken in an instant. Once the "walking dead" himself, surrounded by death, grief, and hopelessness, he has come to realize that since no one knows when their time may come, you must embrace the present and take each day for quite a ride, since it just may be your last.

I have learned to seize the day with gusto. I never allow my loved ones to leave the house without hearing "I love you" since it may be the last words they ever hear from me. I don't allow petty arguments to drag into another day, since another day may not be gifted me. I laugh more than I cry, and when I cry, it is for a good reason but never for long. I give more than I take, and offer more than I accept. Living life, and living it well, shows my gratitude to The One who gives me daily breath.

Love never dies. Neither do your deepest dreams.

People assume that because my husband has remarried, he has, once and forevermore, stopped loving or grieving for his late wife. However, nothing could be further from the truth. It is a wise wife of a widower who accepts that her husband will always hold a special place in his heart for his first love. Grief and love *can* co-exist in the same heart and in the same life.

I have learned that love grows more beautifully as it is shared. It is a never-ending circle. The love my husband's late wife gave to him has helped forge his wonderful heart, which he now shares with me. Therefore, love never really dies.

My husband and his late wife did not have children together, even though it was his deepest desire and fondest dream. When he buried her, he felt that he buried the dream of parenthood along with her, too. But love has a way of righting wrongs and offering hope. Today, he and I are the proud parents of a darling baby girl.

I have learned that every dream is possible, if only we are willing to put our faith where it belongs and let God handle the details.

Take your marriage vows seriously, and to heart

"In sickness and in health...'Til death do us part." Most married folk have uttered these sacred vows to their partners. But how many of us spoke these promises in earnest, thinking that some day, we may have to rise to the occasion?

Newlyweds are too giddy with excitement and hope for their newly joined lives to ever truly imagine that their vows may some day become realities. But these solemn words were written into the marriage ceremony for a reason—to make couples aware that the possibility DOES exist when they may be called upon to stand and deliver.

My husband was his late wife's caregiver during her terminal illness. He changed IV bags, bathed her skeletal, chemotherapy-weakened body, and mopped vomit and blood from the bathroom floor for days on end. He nervously drove her to radiation treatments, and sat heartbroken in waiting rooms full of tired, grief-stricken caregivers who all wore the same ashen, lifeless faces. But he did so not only because he promised to. He did so because, out of love, he wanted to. The bond of intimacy between a dying wife and her loving husband cannot be duplicated, and he wouldn't have missed that for the world.

I have learned that my marriage vows were the most important promises I have ever made…to myself, to my husband, and to God. And out of love for all three, I plan to honor them…'til death do us part.

Something good always comes out of something bad.

Turning negatives into positives takes a great leap of faith. It takes tremendous courage to give up your comfort zone for something less familiar, and often times scarier. But this is what it takes for something good to come from something bad.

The bombing of the World Trade Center on September 11th, 2001 was the most inconceivable tragedy this world has ever known. This deplorable act of terrorism on such a strong and mighty nation could have immobilized the USA with fear. Instead, Americans everywhere pitched in to help their fellow man. And we, as a country, became more aware of the holes in our national defense and allowed us to repair them before another strike catches us unaware.

My husband's loss of his late wife was the most inconceivable tragedy he had ever known. During his subsequent years of grief recovery, he assumed that nothing good would ever happen to him again. Fear had gripped his heart and planted his feet in the ashes of apathy. But today, years after his loss, he has evolved into a new man with a new life and new hopes and dreams for his future. He has remarried, had child of his own, and discovered that it is possible for something good to come out of something bad.

I have learned that when bad things happen, I feel a spark of anticipation for the good things to happen, since they always do. My mother used to tell me that when God closes a door, He always opens a window. The windows in my life have added up to a lot of sunshine, but not before the doors of my past have slammed shut behind me.

You are never alone.

One thing that amazed my husband was how wonderfully friends can rally to your side when tragedy occurs. Although they will never fully understand the pain of loss unless or until it happens to them personally, friends and family are a constant source of comfort in times of need. They will bend over backwards to offer a soothing hug, encouraging words, or an ear to listen, for a while or for as long as you need them.

Still, there were people in my husband's life who showed deep compassion after he lost his wife, but then disappeared as if being in the presence of a mourner was too much for them to bear. There is no lonelier feeling than lying in a empty bed you once shared with the love of your heart, or eating a meal alone at the same table where you once dined with your spouse. The night brings unbearable loneliness when the solitude of a bereaved spouse's new single hood is a constant reminder that he or she is no longer part of a couple.

Missing the company of a spouse what defines grief itself. My husband remembers that awful time in his life, but admits that he never truly felt alone, even as friends dwindled from his life. Knowing his fellowship and friendship with God was the firm foundation of his faith, he believed that the Lord was with him always, blessing him with the peace and comfort he needed to face each sunrise with hope.

I have learned that God never promises to take us *around* the valley of the shadow of death, but *through* it. He knows that to find the light of peace, wisdom, and courage, we must endure the fires of death's sting…but He promises that we will never be alone as we do. God is always with us. We are never alone.

17

ON THE ROAD TO RECOVERY

The old saying is true—time *does* heal all wounds. Not completely, but enough to allow you to feel better about yourself and more hopeful about the future. You will find that as time progresses, you *will* start to feel more hopeful about your husband and your future as a WOW. You *will* start to feel more secure in your marriage. You *will* look back on your early days as a WOW and wonder why you ever felt some of those feelings or thought some of those thoughts in the first place.

Of course, I cannot offer you a money-back guarantee, since life is unpredictable. I'm not saying that all of your WOW issues disappear after a year or two. For some WOWs, it may take that long, and sometimes it may take a lifetime. And some WOWs may never completely resolve *all* of their WOW issues. But one thing is for sure—you *will* reach a point in your life where your negative WOW feelings do not entirely consume you, and will become easier to manage.

You must regard each WOW issue as a challenge, and work on each issue one at a time and day by day. Change does not happen overnight, but with the slow, methodical practice of implementing well-chosen plans. Focus on each issue's relevance in your life and in your marriage. If the issue lacks importance or growth possibilities, then find a way to manage the negativity of it within your defined comfort zone. If resolving the issue is vital to the health of your marriage and/or people that you love, then set your boundaries and stand your ground, even with his friends and family members, past and present.

Get support from and talk openly with the people you trust, since keeping all your WOW anxiety buried deep down inside of you may thrust you headlong into a dangerous depression. Find compromises and solutions together with your husband. Research grief information and become more knowledgeable about your husband's feelings. Recognize the common "grief triggers" in your husband and find a way to be supportive of him without having WOW anxiety quash your intimacy.

Change=Growth

Remember that list of WOW insecurities I listed in Chapter Two? You could probably relate to some or all of them, because most are so common to each and every new WOW. But what I failed to mention (because I wanted you to read the book!) is that these anxieties are *temporary* (or, at least, *should* be)! It is important to recognize growth when it happens, since by doing so, you remain focused on recovery instead of wallowing in the quagmires of negativity and self-doubt. And since change is the catalyst to personal growth, the following are a few examples of healing:

<u>*You know you're getting better when*</u>...

...you *stop* wondering if you'll ever be #1 in "his" heart (because "she" was there first), and start accepting that YOU are the love of his life *now*, since that's what really matters.

...you *stop* feeling guilty about having these petty feelings by recognizing that they are *not* petty if they are important to YOU.

...you *stop* feeling guilty about the selfishness of your feelings by giving yourself permission to "own" your all-too-human emotions.

...you *stop* feeling guilty about living another woman's life (or living the life "she" would be living had she not died) by affirming that it's YOUR life now.

...you *stop* comparing yourself to the late wife by becoming the best person/wife you can be.

…you *stop* thinking that if she walked in the door today, he would run to "her", and you start to assure yourself that with each passing day, your marriage becomes stronger, and the love you share more deeply imbedded in his heart.

…you *stop* thinking that if you and "she" stood side by side and asked him to choose, he would choose "her", and you start growing into a stronger, more confident, and more resilient woman while facing your fears head on.

…you *stop* wondering which songs on the radio were "their" songs, and you start marking memories with songs of your own.

…you *stop* wondering about "their" sex life, and you start making your marital intimacy everything you want it to be.

…you *stop* cringing every time "her" birthday or death anniversary rolls around, and you start detaching and distancing yourself personally from the grief while positively reaffirming your position in your husband's life, empathizing with his plight as you do.

…you *stop* hoping time will make "her" memory fade even more, and you start recognizing that while he may never forget "her", the life you share with your husband is now his first priority.

…you *stop* wondering if he loves you more than he ever loved "her", and you start believing him when he tells you that he loves you, without making him prove it over and over again.

…you *stop* wishing he never met or married "her", and you start appreciating the late wife's contribution to making him the man with whom you fell in love.

…you *stop* wishing he never had to go through so much pain when "she" died, and you start being grateful for the wisdom, growth, and resiliency he learned from the experience.

…you *stop* wondering if he is thinking of "her" when he gets that "far off look" in his eyes, and you start dialoguing with him and communicating your thoughts and fears about his late wife.

...you *no longer* dread going anywhere "they" have been to before since you've acknowledged that the new memories you make together are what are more important.

...you *no longer* dread re-living old memories with "you" playing the role of "her" since you've accepted the fact that your husband did not marry you to clone his late wife.

...you *no longer* dread doing any of the things that "they" used to do, fearing a "grief trigger", since you've learned to confidently embrace your individuality.

...you *stop* hoping your memories together will outshine "theirs", and you become more secure in your husband's love for and devotion to you.

...you *stop* hating "her" just to justify your WOW anxieties, and you start taking more responsibility for your part in the negativity.

...you *stop* wanting to know more about "her", and start to acknowledge that the obsession wasn't helping you deal with your WOW anxieties.

...you *stop* fearing his reaction when asking him about "her", and you start honing your communication skills.

...you *stop* wondering about the possibility of "their" reunion in Heaven and the possibility of no one welcoming you at Heaven's door should they be together before you, and you start learning to live life in the present and not in the unchanging past nor in the ever-changing future.

...you *stop* focusing on his "going" (dying) before you, and you start learning to take each day is it comes and deal with problems ONLY as they arise, thereby avoiding borrowed trouble.

...you *stop* wondering if he would want to be buried beside "her" or beside you, and you start organizing your life by making plans with your husband regarding death-related subjects such as burials and wills.

...you *stop* grousing about not wanting to go through Eternity sharing him with "her", and you start remembering that love is big enough to encompass all of you.

...you *stop* feeling stressed by his grief and your guilt on a daily basis, and you start releasing the burdens you were never meant to bear.

...you *stop* wondering if "she" crosses his mind daily, and you start feeling peaceful about your place in his heart.

You May *Never*...

...stop feeling a little sad for him.

Your husband is the person you care about and love more than anyone else in the world, and no one likes to see the love of their life in painful anguish. Feeling sad shows that you care enough to be sympathetic to his hardships, and allows you to be strong for him during the times when he is somewhat weak with grief.

...stop wondering about the life "they" shared or about the person "she" was.

As long as it is not an obsession that is hell-bent on laying blame, exacting revenge, or making the late wife the enemy, it is quite normal to be curious about the past.

...be accepted by his family or friends, past and present.

If you've tried to work it out, then feel good about yourself in that you gave it your "all". In the future, there will be new friends to make. Understanding the family's grief issues will help you learn to tolerate them better.

...feel totally, 100% comfortable around people who knew "her".

Perhaps you even knew her yourself, but when old friends get together, the weight of their memories of her is just too burdensome for you to bear. You may always wonder if an opportunity for you to be autonomous, apart from any connection to "her" in some way, will ever present itself. Be patient—it will. You will not always be known as a Wife Of a Widower. Some day, you will just be known as "Mrs. So-And-So", or "Mr. So-And-So's wife", without any acknowledgment of the past.

It's Only "Human"

As mentioned earlier in this book, when I was in the research phase of writing my book, I had contacted and communicated with other WOWs (Wives Of Widowers). In order to find a common thread among all of us, I posed questions to each of them regarding what issues they had dealt with as a WOW. Oddly enough, the results of this survey often prompted me to reassure these women by uttering a quasi-patronizing, "That's OK. It's only *human*".

It's only *human* to feel threatened by a ghost who will always reside in your husband's heart.

It's only *human* to feel anxiety on the anniversary date of the late wife's death.

It's only *human* to wonder if your husband will ever love you the way he loved his late wife.

"It's OK. I'm only *human*". That's partially true. I *am* human. And because of this indisputable fact, it only follows that my feelings are human, too. But is it OK to have these feelings of self-doubt, anxiety, and fear?

In a word…no!

I had used this same statement of affirmation on myself when I first married my previously widowed husband. When the old "Insecurity Monster" reared its ugly head and forced me to react negatively or to feel threatened by the late wife's memory and eerie presence in my marriage, I repeated over and over, "What I am feeling is normal—because I'm only *human*, after all". In other words, I excused myself, and by doing so, I had glossed over my fears and allowed them to be pushed aside for the time being. I had not only used this lame excuse to feel better about my negative emotions, but I had also used it to avoid finding a solution to my problematic fears as well.

Why? What was the payoff for my hanging onto my insecurities? Did they benefit my marriage? Did they change the past? Did they make me stronger? Of course not.

As a Christian, I know that negative emotions of fear, anxiety, and self-doubt are NOT of God. They are Satan's tools, and he knows how to operate them put a wedge in your faith and to try to separate what God has joined together.

Yes, all emotions are *human* emotions. After all, Jesus was a human, and felt the negative emotion of fear in the Garden of Gethsemane. However, the big difference between what is human and what is divine was demonstrated by how Jesus handled His anxiety. He went straight to His Father in heaven and asked for strength. He did not stuff his negative emotions into his pocket. Rather, he focused on a solution. And by doing so, He illustrated that that is what He wants us to do, too.

It is easy to do or feel what comes naturally…to do or feel what is *human*. But Christ calls us to do what is spiritual…and divine. He wants us to come unto Him, release our burdens, then be still and know that He will deliver. In Psalm 56:3 (NIV), the Lord speaks through the psalmist and reminds us of this: "*When I am afraid, I put my trust in You*". He wants us to trust our faith and not our humanness.

It would be arrogant for me, either as advice for my fellow WOWs or even for myself, to ever utter the phrase "It's OK…I'm only *human!*" ever again, as if what is human supercedes what is Spirit-directed. My humanity does not solve the problems of fear, anxiety, or insecurity. Most of the time, my humanness only serves to exacerbate my problems.

Of course my human feelings and those of my sister WOWs are real and worthy of mention, perhaps even validation. But when we rely on ourselves—on our *human*ness—to excuse away our negative feelings, we stop putting our trust in God, and the result is a separation from the only One who can comfort, love, and strengthen us out of the darkness of our negative humanity.

In Summary

Remarriage itself is a daunting undertaking, but when one marries someone who has lost a first spouse, it can also be fraught with issues, emotions, and real-life problems that had never before been written about in the history of periodical literature...until now.

Why has such a sensitive relationship and its related subjects been literally ignored for so long? I believe it is because death and death-related issues are still considered "taboo" in today's society. We tend to hold the bereaved sacred and grief hallowed, and rightly so. Still, there are hundreds of books on library and bookstore shelves that address the issues of bereavement. These prove supportive to people who have experienced one of life's greatest tragedies. However, I believe it is now time that we shed some light on an overlooked segment of our society—that of second spouses of the bereaved—since their problems are just as important *within a marriage* as those of a widow or widower.

When my previously widowed husband asked me to marry him, it was, for both of us, a momentous occasion. Not only would we be uniting our two souls, but also two sets of memories, two families...two *pasts*. We would also be joining two sets of "baggage", two broken hearts, and two unique resumes of life experiences.

And as second spouses to the bereaved, we bring all these items to the marriage table, put them in the marital blender, and hope the mixture comes out smooth. With any luck, it will be. But I believe in the power of knowledge and foresight, and I respect the insights of those who speak from experience.

Therefore, and to that end, I wish to offer to all new and/or future brides this "10-Step Guide to Marrying a Widower", based on my own personal experiences and that of my fellow "WOWs" (Wives Of Widowers) with whom I communicated while researching information for my book.

1.   **Embrace the past—Don't hide it or run from it.**

   Ignoring your husband's grief will not stop it. Nothing will. He will most likely forever grieve his loss. Living in denial of grief's existence will only prolong your spouse's grief recovery. Better to allow your husband the opportunities he *requires* to talk about where he's at in his grief journey. Better still to have a relationship where you, too, can talk openly and honestly about your issues regarding his grief and his past, and how they both make you feel about your marriage.

2. **Accept that your marriage will be one of *three* hearts, not two.**

    It's no easy task to share your husband's heart with another woman, but in a marriage to a widower, that is precisely what you must learn to live with. But take heart—it IS possible for grief and love to co-exist! Even more encouraging is the knowledge that your husband's love for his late wife will never diminish what he feels with you!

3. **Don't let pettiness over material possessions get you off on the wrong foot.**

    If you battle with insecurities about whether or not your husband does or will ever love you as much as he loved his late wife, then resenting her pictures or personal possessions from their marriage in your house may seem like an important point of issue to you. Many WOWs deal with this problem when blending two households into one, and it can cause the most pain and frustration in your new marriage—yet it doesn't have to.

    The keys to healing this problem are communication and compromise. Between the two of you, decide which possessions you are both comfortable with keeping, and which of them you are willing to donate to Goodwill. Remember that you each have special mementos of the past that hold great sentimental value. Be sensitive about the other person's feelings when deciding on which of these you can live with if they are to be displayed in your home.

4. **Be ever vigilant about remaining sympathetic and empathetic when dealing with all the bereaved family members.**

    While the late wife's family may or may not accept you into the new extended family fold, remember that they have experienced a great loss and are dealing with the backlash of grief. They may fear that their daughter's/ sister's/niece's/granddaughter's memory will fade into obscurity just because your husband decided to remarry, and may subconsciously blame you for this. If you remain constantly focused on their bereavement, it will become much easier for you to deal with any negativity on their part.

As with anyone who has suffered the loss of a loved one to death, allow them their memories and be patient as they learn to grow to love who *you* are and respect your place in your husband's life.

5. **Don't dwell on the past or let it feed your insecurities.**

    Was the late wife prettier/sexier/funnier than you? Was she a better cook/lover/friend/parent/etc.? Comparisons are normal, yet when we fall short of our own comparisons, they can feed our insecurities and inhibit the growth of a relationship with a spouse.

    Your husband did not marry you because you were an exact replica or clone of his late wife. He, more than anyone else, is keenly aware of the unique and special qualities that made him fall in love with you, no matter how different or alike they are in comparison to his first wife. Accept that you and the late wife are two different people, both with wonderful characteristics that are worthy of your husband's love. Remember that the negative differences you create in your own failed comparison to the late wife may be just the reasons why your husband found you to be so appealing!

6. **Be selfless and gracious enough to accommodate grief-related episodes as they occur.**

    You cannot love a widower enough to make him forget his late wife. Yes, time is a healer, and along every grief journey, sadness turns to joy at some point. However, do not be fooled into thinking that your husband's late wife's death anniversary or their wedding anniversary, her birthday, or holidays will be grief-free.

    He may be unwilling to share his grief feelings with you on these special occasions simply because he may be afraid that speaking of them will hurt your feelings. These are the times to boldly take the bull by the horns and graciously offer your permission as well as your understanding. Lovingly remind him that you are aware of the significance of these dates when they occur, and that you are available to listen should he wish to share his feelings. Also, offer to go with him to the cemetery if that is what he desires. As painful as it may seem, joining your husband in this way can be soul cleansing to both of you and to your marriage because of the opportunity for therapeutically honest communication that arises.

7. **Firmly set boundaries, but with gentleness and cooperation.**

A marriage to a widower isn't all about his grief and tiptoeing gently around it. YOUR feelings matter, too, and they deserve validation, no matter how petty, insensitive (to grief), and unrealistic the outside world may find them.

Many WOWs are hurt when their husbands refer to their late wives as "my first wife" or simply "my wife, Hazel (or whatever her name was!)". If you can relate to this issue, you must firmly but gently communicate your discomfort to your husband, and allow him the opportunity to be as sensitive to your "second wife needs" as you are to his "grief needs".

8. **Read, research, and learn all you can about the stages of grief and what to expect from each.**

By the time you marry, most of your husband's grief journey will be complete. However, as with all bereaved persons, there will always remain a spark of grief that must be dealt with on a regular basis. If you are to be truly "one" with your husband, it will be your responsibility to learn all you can about grief and its effects in order to understand how they will eventually fit into your individual marital puzzles.

Dr. Elizabeth Kubler-Ross has penned a wonderful book based on her study of the bereaved called "On Death And Dying". In it, she outlines the stages of grief, and what a bereaved person can expect from each. While the book falls short of fully describing the remarriage of widows and widowers, it is a wonderful reference to absorb should you wish to become better informed about the journey of bereavement and of your husband's heart.

9. **Don't be afraid to seek outside help should you find your WOW feelings to be overwhelmingly frustrating.**

My husband and I shared a very special communication about his past, his late wife, and his feelings about both, which provided comfort and encouragement to both of us in our marriage. However, at times I still tended to tilt at the windmills of my mind as well as the intimidating ghostly presence of his late wife.

Wives of widowers are few and far between, and sometimes, we aren't even aware of whom our WOW sisters are! They could be our neighbors, our chatty friends at Yoga class, or even the mothers of our children's friends. Our WOW status and the issues that arise because of it are not the typical conversation fodder for most casual acquaintances! Therefore, we do not have a social circle of supportive friends to whom we can share, vent, and discuss our mutual WOW angst and joys.

So many WOWs feel that they are either alone in their feelings, or just a tad crazy to have them at all! Therefore, it becomes acutely necessary for a WOW who constantly deals with negative pressures of her role to seek the support of a counselor, clergyman, or fellow WOW. Sometimes, just getting validation for our distinctive WOW emotions is the first step towards healing them.

10. **Live for the present and welcome the future by making each day count.**

Every day of life you live and every breath you take are gifts from God. Show your appreciation by making each of them count! Make new memories with your husband that are special only to the two of you and that are autonomous from his marriage to his late wife.

Plan vacations to exotic places that neither of you has ever visited. Combine your holiday traditions, thereby making new ones that will become unique to your marriage. Redecorate your house or even one room at a time together, or buy a new home—together—and make it your *own*.

Life is a teacher, so be a good student. Study, pay attention, and ask questions. Remember—you cannot change the past, but you *can* accommodate, accept, and yes, even embrace its memory without sacrificing the quality of your present and/or future life.

18

WHEN ALL ELSE FAILS

If you have read this book and still feel that your WOW problems seem hopelessly insurmountable, keep in mind that just like grief, your problems *will* diminish with time. It may look like an enormous mountain of work and stresses to iron out, but what marriage *ISN'T* hard work? Your courage, strength, fortitude, and perseverance are admirable, and if you want to continue to find resources to help you through the WOW experience, then you've come to the right place!

Counseling

If you are a WOW stepmother and are finding your husband's children are acting out their grief issues in negative or destructive ways, I strongly recommend Rainbows International (web site: **http://www.rainbows.org**). This wonderful peer support group (group therapy) counseling service is for children of separation, either by death or divorce. Rainbow groups are run by highly trained facilitators—sometimes lay people, and sometimes child psychologists—and every session is geared to a child's level, making them a lot of fun for the kids, too! Look at their web site for more information and to find a local chapter. The best part of Rainbows is—it's free!

If there are no Rainbows International sessions near you, then I urge you to contact a child psychologist who specializes in separation issues. Don't worry about his or her fee—most work on a sliding scale according to your income, and many insurance companies will now cover therapy fees. Children are deeply affected by the death of a natural parent, and unfortunately, loving them as a

WOW is just not enough to help them through their pain, insecurity, and confusion.

If you and your husband are considering marriage counseling, or if you are considering individual counseling just for yourself, then I support your decision 100%! Therapy is NOT an experience of which you should be ashamed. In fact, I find that most couples that attend counseling sessions regularly are brave, mature, and wise. They want to find out what is causing their problems and find a way to repair the damage before it's too late.

Nothing wrong with that! It helps tremendously to have an impartial third party analyze your marriage's (or individual) strengths and weaknesses, and then help guide you through the healing process. I found that the marriage counseling my husband and I attended was a breakthrough in the area of intimacy, in that we learned how to strengthen our communication skills and acquired the tools needed to implement positive changes.

You may also find your church to be of great comfort to you, as well as an excellent source of counseling opportunities, no matter what your religion. Ministers, priests, rabbis, and other church leaders are well trained in the area of bereavement and marital counseling, whether you are affiliated with their church or not.

Information On Understanding Grief

As I have said many times in this book, I highly recommend researching the subject of grief in order that you might be more empathetic to the enormous emotional upheaval that your husband has endured by losing a spouse to death. By doing so, you will find it easier to cope with those times when his Grief Monster makes an appearance, and will allow you to grow as a more sympathetic and selfless partner.

My favorite book about grief is the classic, "On Death And Dying", by Dr. Elizabeth Kubler-Ross. It is one of the most important psychological studies of the late twentieth century, and grew out of Dr. Kubler-Ross's famous interdisciplinary seminar on death, life, and transition. In this remarkable book, Dr. Kübler-Ross first explored the now-famous "five stages of death": denial and isolation, anger, bargaining, depression, and acceptance. Especially educational and heart-wrenchingly honest are the excerpts of her interviews with the participants of her studies.

If your husband was his wife's caretaker during her terminal illness, then C.S. Lewis's book, "<u>A Grief Observed</u>", will help you to comprehend just what a tragic and difficult journey grief is. Mr. Lewis's own wife died of cancer, and in his book, he poignantly writes a very anguished, luminous essay about the meaning of death, marriage, and religion. As his late wife's caretaker, my husband can relate to everything Mr. Lewis writes in this first-hand account of his own personal grief journey.

Of course, there are thousands of books dealing with the subject of grief, but these are my best recommendations. I urge you to visit your local library or bookstores (online bookstores are a great resource!) for further information.

Internet Resources

There are several grief support groups online that are excellent resources for understanding grief, and may be beneficial to your husband in his grief recovery as well, but rarely do these sites offer support for WOWs, so be careful upon entering their domain. You will be dealing with people who have experienced loss, not remarriage, so be respectful if you have a question for the widow/ers who post to these sites. It is always a good idea to first look at the site owner's TOS (terms of service), to see if you are, in fact, welcome to post to his/her site's message board or participate in a chat room discussions as a non-widowed person.

Several interesting web sites dealing with grief are the following:

Grief Loss and Bereavement Counseling Site Online
(**<u>http://www.angelfire.com/hi5/memories0/</u>**)*

GROWW—Grief Recovery Online
(**<u>http://www.groww.org/</u>**)*

ShareGrief.com Online Grief Counseling
(**<u>http://www.sharegrief.com/our_counsellor.html/</u>**)*

GriefNet.org—A Community of Persons Dealing With Grief
(**http://www.griefnet.org/**)*

(*At the time of this writing, these web sites were all operational. I apologize for your inconvenience if any of them have been disabled since this book was printed.)

One-On-One WOW Support

I invite you to please visit my web site (**http://www.authorsden.com/juliedonnerandersen**) if you'd like to post a question for me to try and answer. I will attempt to reply to everyone's inquiries, but I cannot guarantee a personal response. My web site is also a great resource for interesting WOW and widower articles, WOWs in the news, grief information, and a WOW message board where you can meet other WOWs from all over the world to discuss mutual WOW interests and issues.

I hope to see you there!

THE END

0-595-27480-3

CPSIA information can be obtained
at www.ICGtesting.com
Printed in the USA
LVOW08s2023181217

560203LV00008B/731/P